TEEN RIGHTS AND FREEDOMS

| Religion

Teen Rights and Freedoms

I Religion

Noël Merino
Book Editor

GREENHAVEN PRESS
A part of Gale, Cengage Learning

GALE
CENGAGE Learning·

Detroit • New York • San Francisco • New Haven, Conn • Waterville, Maine • London

Elizabeth Des Chenes, *Managing Editor*

© 2012 Greenhaven Press, a part of Gale, Cengage Learning

Gale and Greenhaven Press are registered trademarks used herein under license.

For more information, contact:
Greenhaven Press
27500 Drake Rd.
Farmington Hills, MI 48331-3535
Or you can visit our Internet site at gale.cengage.com.

For product information and technology assistance, contact us at:

Gale Customer Support, 1-800-877-4253.
For permission to use material from this text or product, submit all requests online at www.cengage.com/permissions.

Further permissions questions can be emailed to permissionrequest@cengage.com.

Articles in Greenhaven Press anthologies are often edited for length to meet page requirements. In addition, original titles of these works are changed to clearly present the main thesis and to explicitly indicate the author's opinion. Every effort is made to ensure the Greenhaven Press accurately reflects the original intent of the authors. Every effort has been made to trace the owners of copyrighted material.

Cover Image © George Muresan/Shutterstock.com.

LIBRARY OF CONGRESS CATALOGING-IN-PUBLICATION DATA

Religion / Noël Merino, book editor.
    p. cm. -- (Teen rights and freedoms)
    Includes bibliographical references and index.
    ISBN 978-0-7377-5831-3 (hardcover : alk. paper)
  1. Religion in the public schools--Law and legislation--United States. 2. Prayer in the public schools--Law and legislation--United States. 3. Freedom of religion--United States. 4. Freedom of speech--United States. 5. United States. Supreme Court. I. Merino, Noël.
    KF4162.W485 2011
    344.73'0796--dc22

                                                                        2011015668

Printed in the United States of America
1 2 3 4 5 6 7 15 14 13 12 11

Contents

Hugo Black

The US Supreme Court concluded that any state law requiring public schoolchildren to recite a religious prayer violates the Establishment Clause of the First Amendment.

Tom C. Clark

The US Supreme Court concludes that reading passages from the Bible in public school is a violation of the First Amendment demand that the government not advance any particular religion.

David Niose

A lawyer interviews one of the student plaintiffs from the 1963 *Abington Township v. Schempp* case, who defends the continued separation of church and state.

Kent Demaret

A journalist reports that one of the student plaintiffs from the 1963 US Supreme Court case disallowing religious practices now regrets his involvement in the case and supports school prayer.

Warren E. Burger

The US Supreme Court finds that requiring school after the eighth grade may be unconstitutional if it interferes with the free exercise of religion, such as with the Amish.

Per Curiam *opinion*

The US Supreme Court contends that displaying the Ten Commandments in public school classrooms, even if financed privately, violates the First Amendment.

John Paul Stevens

The US Supreme Court determined that a state statute authorizing a moment of silence in public schools was unconstitutional because the intent was to promote voluntary prayer.

Anthony Kennedy

The US Supreme Court ruled that public school officials may not allow a religious leader to give a nonsectarian prayer at a school event where there is a captive audience, such as graduation.

John Paul Stevens

The US Supreme Court ruled that a school policy allowing a prayer at football games, led by a student who was elected by other students, is unconstitutional.

Cathy Young

A writer contends that secularists want religious speech to be restricted and anti-secularists want speech against religion to be restricted, showing neither wants truly free speech about religion.

Nat Hentoff

A writer claims that the US Supreme Court is not doing an adequate job of protecting the First Amendment rights of students when their expression has a religious component.

Rob Boston

The assistant director of communications for Americans United for Separation of Church and State argues that people need to remain vigilant against religion in public schools.

Foreword

*"In the truest sense freedom cannot be
bestowed, it must be achieved."*
Franklin D. Roosevelt,
September 16, 1936

The notion of children and teens having rights is a relatively recent development. Early in American history, the head of the household—nearly always the father—exercised complete control over the children in the family. Children were legally considered to be the property of their parents. Over time, this view changed, as society began to acknowledge that children have rights independent of their parents, and that the law should protect young people from exploitation. By the early twentieth century, more and more social reformers focused on the welfare of children, and over the ensuing decades advocates worked to protect them from harm in the workplace, to secure public education for all, and to guarantee fair treatment for youths in the criminal justice system. Throughout the twentieth century, rights for children and teens—and restrictions on those rights—were established by Congress and reinforced by the courts. Today's courts are still defining and clarifying the rights and freedoms of young people, sometimes expanding those rights and sometimes limiting them. Some teen rights are outside the scope of public law and remain in the realm of the family, while still others are determined by school policies.

Each volume in the Teen Rights and Freedoms series focuses on a different right or freedom and offers an anthology of key essays and articles on that right or freedom and the responsibilities that come with it. Material within each volume is drawn from a diverse selection of primary and secondary sources—journals, magazines, newspapers, nonfiction books, organization newsletters, position papers, speeches, and government documents, with a particular emphasis on Supreme Court and lower court decisions. Volumes also include first-person narratives from young people and others involved in teen rights issues, such as parents and educators. The material is selected and arranged to highlight all the major social and legal controversies relating to the right or freedom under discussion. Each selection is preceded by an introduction that provides context and background. In many cases, the essays point to the difference between adult and teen rights, and why this difference exists.

Many of the volumes cover rights guaranteed under the Bill of Rights and how these rights are interpreted and protected in regard to children and teens, including freedom of speech, freedom of the press, due process, and religious rights. The scope of the series also encompasses rights or freedoms, whether real or perceived, relating to the school environment, such as electronic devices, dress, Internet policies, and privacy. Some volumes focus on the home environment, including topics such as parental control and sexuality.

Numerous features are included in each volume of Teen Rights and Freedoms:

- An annotated **table of contents** provides a brief summary of each essay in the volume and highlights court decisions and personal narratives.
- An **introduction** specific to the volume topic gives context for the right or freedom and its impact on daily life.
- A brief **chronology** offers important dates associated with the right or freedom, including landmark court cases.
- **Primary sources**—including personal narratives and court decisions—are among the varied selections in the anthology.
- **Illustrations**—including photographs, charts, graphs, tables, statistics, and maps—are closely tied to the text and chosen to help readers understand key points or concepts.

- An annotated list of **organizations to contact** presents sources of additional information on the topic.

- A **for further reading** section offers a bibliography of books, periodical articles, and Internet sources for further research.

- A comprehensive subject **index** provides access to key people, places, events, and subjects cited in the text.

Each volume of Teen Rights and Freedoms delves deeply into the issues most relevant to the lives of teens: their own rights, freedoms, and responsibilities. With the help of this series, students and other readers can explore from many angles the evolution and current expression of rights both historic and contemporary.

Introduction

The First Amendment to the US Constitution guarantees, "Congress shall make no law respecting an establishment of religion, or prohibiting the exercise thereof." The first clause, known as the Establishment Clause, prohibits the government from establishing or endorsing any official religion. The second clause, known as the free exercise clause, prohibits the government from limiting the exercise of religion through belief, speech, or conduct. Together, these clauses form the foundation of religious freedom in the United States. In the two centuries since the adoption of the First Amendment, the US Supreme Court has played a key role in interpreting, defining, and delineating how these two clauses apply to religious freedom in daily life, both for adults and minors.

The Establishment Clause guarantees what has come to be known as the separation of church and state. The idea of "building a wall of separation between church and State" comes from a letter to the Danbury Baptist Association in 1802 by Thomas Jefferson. The Court's foremost case defining this separation of church and state under the Establishment Clause is *Lemon v. Kurtzman* (1971). At issue in *Lemon* was state financial support for parochial—that is, private religious—schools and their teachers. In finding the particular financial support at issue in this case to be unconstitutional, the Court articulated three elements necessary for a law, or statute, to be constitutional under the Establishment Clause: "First, the statute must have a secular legislative purpose; second, its principal or primary effect must be one that neither advances nor inhibits religion; . . . finally, the statute must not foster an excessive government entanglement with religion." The *Lemon* test, as it has come to be known, continues to be used in the courts, though not without debate concerning what the test allows and disallows.

The Free Exercise Clause guarantees that the government may not prohibit the exercise of religion. The exercise of one's religion may involve belief, speech, and conduct, but as the Court recognized early on: "The Amendment embraces two concepts—freedom to believe and freedom to act. The first is absolute, but, in the nature of things, the second cannot be."[1] Thus, whereas the right to freedom of religious belief is absolute, the right to engage in religious speech and conduct is not. The Free Speech Clause of the First Amendment helps to support the freedom of religious expression but, as with all expression, this right is not absolute. The Court's first decision regarding the Free Exercise Clause illustrates this distinction between belief and conduct. In *Reynolds v. United States* (1878), the Court held that the Free Exercise Clause does not protect the right to engage in polygamy—marrying more than one spouse—even if one's religion demands the practice:

> Laws are made for the government of actions, and while they cannot interfere with mere religious belief and opinions, they may with practices. Suppose one believed that human sacrifices were a necessary part of religious worship; would it be seriously contended that the civil government under which he lived could not interfere to prevent a sacrifice?

Thus, the free exercise of religion may be limited by the government in situations where religious conduct is seen as harming others or otherwise at odds with legitimate government interests.

The arena in which the religious freedom of minors is most pertinent is within the public schools. The First Amendment's guarantees of freedom from government establishment of religion and free exercise of religion apply to public schools, as elsewhere. In *Lee v. Weisman* (1992), the Court noted that the public school context was one in which the state must be particularly careful about establishing or endorsing religion: "What to most believers may seem nothing more than a reasonable request that the nonbeliever respect their religious practices, in a school context may appear to the nonbeliever or dissenter to be an attempt to employ the machinery of the State to enforce a religious orthodoxy." Based on the Establishment Clause, the Court has held that public schools may not engage in religious teachings, school prayer, Bible reading (except as literature), posting of religious material such as the Ten Commandments, or suppression of the teaching of evolution in order to promote religious theories.

Even though the Court has held that public schools may not sponsor religious activities, the Court has recognized that the Free Exercise Clause of the First Amendment protects the rights of students to engage in private religious activity at school. One of the areas in which the Court has protected the exercise of religion by minors is as it relates to student clubs. In *Board of Education of Westside Community Schools v. Mergens* (1990), the Court ruled that public schools may not prevent student religious groups from forming clubs or using school grounds in the same manner as any other noncurriculum club. The Court has noted, "There is a crucial difference between government speech endorsing religion, which the Establishment Clause forbids, and private speech endorsing religion, which the Free Speech and Free Exercise Clauses protect." Thus, as long as student religious activity at school is private, it is protected.

Just how one ought to understand the guarantee of religious freedom in the Bill of Rights continues to be a source of controversy, and one of the key places where this debate plays out is in the public schools. Some believe that the Court has gone too far in eliminating religion from public schools, whereas others believe it has not gone far enough. Some of the key Court decisions regarding the religious freedom of teens, primarily within the context of public school, and commentary about the direction of the Court are explored in *Teen Rights and Freedoms: Religion.*

Note

1. *Cantwell v. Connecticut*, 310 US 296 (1940).

Chronology

1791

The Bill of Rights was adopted by the United States, of which the First Amendment reads: "Congress shall make no law respecting an establishment of religion, or prohibiting the free exercise thereof; or abridging the freedom of speech, or of the press; or the right of the people peaceably to assemble, and to petition the Government for a redress of grievances."

1925

In *Pierce v. Society of Sisters* the Supreme Court declares unconstitutional an Oregon law that forced all children to attend public schools rather than parochial schools.

1940

In *Minersville School District v. Gobitis* the Supreme Court rules that the rights of Jehovah's Witnesses were not violated when they were required to salute the flag in public schools.

1943

In *West Virginia State Board of Education v. Barnette* the Supreme Court reverses the *Minersville School District v. Gobitis* decision, claiming that a compulsory salute of the American flag by schoolchildren violates the First Amendment.

1947

In *Everson v. Board of Education of Ewing Township* the Supreme Court incorporates the Establishment Clause of the First Amendment into state constitutions, forbidding states from establishing an official religion.

1948

In *McCollum v. Board of Education* the Supreme Court declares unconstitutional a Champaign, Illinois, program that allowed religious teachers into public schools to teach about religion.

1952

In *Zorach v. Clauson* the Supreme Court rules that New York City is entitled to allow students to be excused from classes for religious instruction as long as the students go off campus.

1962

In *Engel v. Vitale* the Supreme Court determines that prayers in public school must be banned even if they are denominationally neutral.

1963

In *Abington Township School District v. Schempp* the Supreme Court strikes down Pennsylvania's requirement that Bible verses be read daily, without comment, in public schools.

1968

In *Epperson v. Arkansas* the Supreme Court holds that a 1928 Arkansas law that prohibited the teaching of evolution in public schools is unconstitutional.

1971   In *Lemon v. Kurtzman* the Supreme Court rules unconstitutional certain tax-supported programs that aid private religious schools.

1972   In *Wisconsin v. Yoder* the Supreme Court rules that Amish children may leave school after eighth grade because to require attendance offends their right to free exercise of religion.

1973   In *Committee for Public Education and Religious Liberty v. Nyquist* the Supreme Court finds unconstitutional a program supporting tuition tax credits for low-income parents wanting to send their children to parochial schools.

1980   In *Stone v. Graham* the Supreme Court holds that posting the Ten Commandments in public school classrooms is in violation of the First Amendment.

1985   In *Grand Rapids School District v. Ball* the Supreme Court rules unconstitutional a program in which teachers are paid by the state to come to church schools to teach various subjects.

1985   In *Wallace v. Jaffree* the Supreme Court rules that an Alabama policy requiring a moment of silence for meditation or voluntary prayer in public schools violates the Establishment Clause of the First Amendment.

1987
In *Edwards v. Aguillard* the Supreme Court strikes down a Louisiana act requiring evolution and creation science to be taught together, saying that it violates the Establishment Clause of the First Amendment.

1990
In *Board of Education of Westside Community Schools v. Mergens* the Supreme Court rules that public high schools must allow religious groups to meet on campus as long as the schools allow noncurricular clubs in general.

1992
In *Lee v. Weisman* the Supreme Court rules that prayers by clergy at public school graduation ceremonies are unconstitutional.

1993
In *Lamb's Chapel v. Center Moriches Union Free School District* the Supreme Court rules that it is unconstitutional for states to restrict the after-hours use of public school property to prevent religious-oriented material.

2000
In *Santa Fe Independent School District v. Doe* the Supreme Court holds that public school students may not vote to select speakers who offer prayers at the beginning of football games.

2001   In *Good News Club v. Milford Central School* the Supreme Court rules that a private Christian organization may use public school facilities along with secular groups.

2002   In *Zelman v. Simmons-Harris* the Supreme Court rules that it is not unconstitutional for a state to offer a school voucher program that pays tuition for low-income students in religious schools.

2004   In *Locke v. Davey* the Supreme Court rules that it is not unconstitutional for a state to offer a scholarship program that excludes students who pursue a course of study that is devotional in nature.

> "*The conscious decision to create separation between church and state . . . continues to make the U.S. constitutional experience distinctive.*"

The Establishment Clause of the First Amendment Guarantees Freedom from State Religion

Marci Hamilton

In the following viewpoint Marci Hamilton claims the Establishment Clause of the First Amendment prevents the government from establishing any official religion, resulting in the separation between church and state. Hamilton contends that the US Supreme Court does not have a simple test for determining what kind of activity amounts to the establishment of religion, but she points out some key cases that have helped the Court define its understanding of the First Amendment. She argues that the Establishment Clause was behind the Court's rejection of a Ten Commandments display in a public school classroom and school prayer in public school. Nonetheless, she claims that the Establishment Clause does not prevent all religion in public life, as the Free Exercise Clause of the First Amendment prevents the government from prohibiting

Marci Hamilton, *Encyclopedia of the Supreme Court of the United States*. Belmont, CA: Macmillan Reference USA, 2008. Copyright © 2008 Macmillan Reference USA. Reproduced by permission of Gale, a part of Cengage Learning.

the free exercise of one's religion. Hamilton is the Paul R. Verkuil Chair in Public Law at the Benjamin N. Cardozo School of Law at Yeshiva University.

The First Amendment to the U.S. Constitution contains two clauses related to religion. The first is the *establishment clause* and the second is the *free exercise clause*. The establishment clause provides: "Congress shall make no law respecting an establishment of religion."

The U.S. Supreme Court's establishment clause jurisprudence has been a very context-dependent doctrine. There is no single formula for all cases implicating the separation of church and state, and no attempt by the Court to create one. The doctrine can be categorized into several discrete categories, including government aid to religion, taxation of religion, government support or endorsement of religion, religion in the public schools, and delegation of government authority to religious entities.

The Separation Between Church and State

One of the more interesting developments in American constitutional history is the turn from state establishments to the contemporary era where a state (or national) establishment of any single religion is virtually unthinkable. Before the Bill of Rights was added to the Constitution in 1791 and the disestablishment principle was introduced into American constitutional jurisprudence, a number of the early states established a particular religion, which included the power to tax proceeds and special privileges. In general, the established churches were religious organizations that had escaped the coercive, established churches of Europe. Ironically, they instituted their own establishments on the other side of the Atlantic. To quote President William Howard Taft (1857–1930), the Massachusetts Puritans "came to this country to establish freedom of their religion, and not the freedom of anybody else's religion."

In a similar vein, the Supreme Court has described the impetus for the establishment clause in the case of *Everson v. Board of Education of Ewing* (1947) as follows:

> A large proportion of the early settlers of this country came here from Europe to escape the bondage of laws which compelled them to support and attend government favored churches. . . . [State-established churches repeated] many of the old world practices and persecutions. . . . The people . . . reached the conviction that individual religious liberty could be achieved best under a government which was stripped of all power to tax, to support, or otherwise to assist any or all religions.

James Madison (1751–1836), who drafted the First Amendment, expressed the view in 1785 that not "even three pence" of tax proceeds should be used to support religious teaching. He further explained: "It degrades from the equal rank of Citizens all those whose opinions in Religion do not bend to those of the Legislative authority. Distant as it may be in its present form from the Inquisition, it differs from it only in degree. The one is the first step, the other the last in the career of intolerance."

Some of the strongest proponents of disestablishment principles at the time of the founding and then the framing were those religious entities that had experienced suppression at the hands of the American established churches. The Baptists, in particular, fought for a separation between church and state after their experiences of oppression by the Congregationalists in Massachusetts. Thomas Jefferson, a deist, also railed against the government establishment of religion in the most famous statement about American disestablishment in history, which appeared in his January 1, 1802, letter to the Danbury Baptists.

> Believing with you that religion is a matter which lies solely between man and his God, that he owes account to none other for his faith or his worship, that the legislative powers of

In 2003 a federal judge ordered the removal of a monument of the Ten Commandments erected outside of West Union High School in West Union, Ohio. In Stone v. Graham *(1980) the Supreme Court held as unconstitutional statutes that mandate such displays in public schools.* © AP Images/Al Behrman.

government reach actions only, and not opinions, I contemplate with sovereign reverence that act of the whole American people which declared that their legislature would "make no law respecting an establishment of religion, or prohibiting the free exercise thereof," thus building a wall of separation between church and state.

The "wall" metaphor has been criticized in many corners for overstating the inability of church and state to work together, but it has been an enduring characterization of the intended relationship between church and state. According to the Court, "some limited and incidental entanglement between church and state authority is inevitable in a complex modern society . . . but the concept of a 'wall' of separation is a useful signpost" [*Larkin v. Grendel's Den* (1982)].

The Court's Understanding of the Establishment Clause

There is no "grand unified theory" of the establishment clause, to quote Justice Sandra Day O'Connor's concurring opinion in *Board of Educ. of Kiryas Joel Village School Dist. v. Grumet*. She further explained, "Experience proves that the Establishment Clause, like the Free Speech Clause, cannot easily be reduced to a single test. There are different categories of Establishment Clause cases, which may call for different approaches." The inability to reduce establishment issues to a neat formula has not stopped the Court from deciding a wide array of issues, from the public posting of the Ten Commandments or crèche displays to the use of government aid for many educational purposes.

For some justices, though, like Justice Antonin Scalia, who prefer a bright-line approach to the law, the Court's establishment clause jurisprudence has been a source of frustration.

The Court's leading disestablishment case, and its most criticized, is *Lemon v. Kurtzman* (1971). Under *Lemon*, the Court looked at three factors to determine constitutionality: "first, the statute must have a secular legislative purpose; second, its principal or primary effect must be one that neither advances nor inhibits religion; . . . finally, the statute must not foster an excessive government entanglement with religion." These principles have endured, despite criticism, though the third factor—excessive entanglement—has, at times, been treated as a subcategory of the second—principal or primary effect.

Religion and Public Education

Prior to World War II (1939–1945), the U.S. Supreme Court had not considered the matter of religion and American public education. The prevailing view of the U.S. Constitution was that the religion clauses (establishment and free exercise) of the First Amendment applied to the federal government, not state governments. . . . The Court increasingly applied greater portions of the First Amendment to the states in light of the Fourteenth Amendment's due process clause. In doing so, the Court laid the foundation for considering prayers in public schools. By the time the Court took up this question, religious activities were widespread in public education, especially in the South and Northeast. Such religious activities included school-sponsored prayer (33 percent), Gideon Bible distribution, Christmas concerts, and prayers at commencement exercises or baccalaureate services.

Bruce J. Dierenfield, "School Prayer,"
Encyclopedia of the Supreme Court of
the United States, 2008.

Depending on the context, the Court also has applied other more specific tests, which are refinements of the approach summarized in *Lemon,* including a non-endorsement test, which Justice O'Connor introduced in her concurrence to *Lynch v. Donnelly* (1984), where she explained that "endorsement sends a message to nonadherents that they are outsiders, not full members of the political community, and an accompanying message to adherents that they are insiders, favored members of the political community." The Court also has applied a test in the public school context that forbids "subtle" or "indirect" coercion of students to participate in a religious observance, a test that is very close in tenor and result to the non-endorsement test [*Lee v. Weisman* (1992)]. The Court explained: "What to most believers may seem nothing more than a reasonable request that the nonbeliever respect their religious practices, in a school context may appear to the nonbeliever or dissenter to be an attempt to employ the machinery of the State to enforce a religious orthodoxy." In *Mitchell v. Helms* (2000), four members of the Court (Chief Justice William Rehnquist and Justices Clarence Thomas, Antonin Scalia, and Anthony Kennedy) championed a more robust anticoercion test that would permit significantly more state-sponsored religious observance and aid.

Religion in Public Schools

The first government aid case involving schools was *Everson*, which addressed whether New Jersey could provide school buses for all students, whether they attended public or private schools. The challenge was based on the fact that the vast majority of the students in the private schools receiving the benefit attended parochial schools. The Court upheld the funding, because the program "does no more than provide a general program to help parents get their children, regardless of their religion, safely and expeditiously to and from [state] accredited schools."

Subsequent cases have upheld government funding for textbooks, computers, school vouchers, and special education teachers on the premises of a private school; among other funding possibilities. . . .

In addition to the question whether the government may provide monetary or goods aid to religious entities, the Court has spent a great deal of time and effort drawing the boundary lines for government support or endorsement of religious symbols and messages. . . .

Several cases have raised the question whether the government may sponsor a display of the Ten Commandments in public. In 1980 the Court held that a Kentucky statute mandating the display of the Ten Commandments on public school classroom walls was unconstitutional, because there was no secular purpose behind the posting. According to the Court in *Stone v. Graham* (1980), "the preeminent purpose for posting the Ten

Commandments on schoolroom walls is plainly religious in nature. The Ten Commandments are undeniably a sacred text in the Jewish and Christian faiths, and no legislative recitation of a supposed secular purpose can blind us to that fact." . . .

Despite persistent public pressure from some corners, it is now well-settled that a public school may not lead prayer within the school. In *Engel v. Vitale* (1962), the Court rejected the New York State Board of Regents' requirement that mandated daily prayer in public schools. Six (out of seven) members of the Court found that this was a violation of the establishment clause, because "the constitutional prohibition against laws respecting an establishment of religion must at least mean that in this country it is no part of the business of government to compose official prayers for any group of the American people to recite as a part of a religious program carried on by government." Nor may a school sponsor or endorse a prayer by a member of the clergy at graduation or create and endorse a system for students to deliver prayers at football games, as decided respectively in the cases of *Santa Fe Independent School District v. Doe* (2000) and *Lee v. Weisman* (1992).

Students, however, may use school grounds and buildings for their own, after-school religious observance when the school has opened its facilities to other extracurricular activities, a decision that was reached with *Board of Educ. [of Westside Community Schools] v. Mergens* (1990) and *Lamb's Chapel v. Center Moriches Union Free Sch. Dist.* (1993), so long as the school or school authorities are not endorsing the religious message of the group. . . .

The Bill of Rights, including the First Amendment, is directed at the national government that was crafted by the framers. There is no corresponding Bill of Rights that would be applied against the states. The Court, however, has interpreted the Fourteenth Amendment as "incorporating" certain of the rights referenced in the Bill of Rights against the states. The Court has consistently found that the religion clauses are incorporated by the Fourteenth Amendment and, therefore, apply to state and local government.

MAJOR RELIGIOUS TRADITIONS IN THE US

	Among all adults %
Christian	**78.4**
Protestant	51.3
Catholic	23.9
Mormon	1.7
Jehovah's Witness	0.7
Orthodox	0.6
Other Christian	0.3
Other Religions	**4.7**
Jewish	1.7
Buddhist	0.7
Muslim	0.6
Hindu	0.4
Other World Religions	<0.3
Other Faiths	1.2
Unaffiliated	**16.1**
Don't Know/Refused	**0.8**
	100

Note: Due to rounding, figures may not add to 100 and nested figures may not add to the subtotal indicated.

Taken from: "US Religious Landscape Survey," Pew Forum on Religion & Public Life, February 2008.

The Court in *Everson* held that the Fourteenth Amendment incorporates the establishment clause against the states, reasoning that incorporation of the establishment clause is just as worthy of incorporation as the free exercise clause had been in previous cases. The result is that local and state governments, as well as the federal government, have been required to observe disestablishment principles. . . .

Religious Liberty in the United States

The Court's establishment clause doctrine is not nearly as neat or orderly as the Court's free exercise doctrine. In part, the difficulty lies in the fact that the disestablishment cases ask the Court to draw the boundaries of power between church and state, a task similar in important respects to the difficult charting of boundaries between the branches of government. Some have argued that establishment clause doctrine can and should be simplified to embody only the principle of religious liberty, a doctrine that would dramatically increase the opportunities for government aid and support of religion. As of 2008, the Supreme Court had declined to reduce disestablishment to any single principle, including liberty.

The doctrine's imprecise borders [have] at times led school districts and local governments to worry about whether their holiday displays or activities cross the establishment clause line. It seems clear, though, that so long as the school or government is not clearly endorsing a single religious tradition but rather has some secular purpose for the holiday activity, it will be upheld. Thus, a public school's choral concert that includes both Christmas and Hanukkah music is likely to pass muster, while a classroom party that revolves around reading the biblical version of Christ's birth is more at risk. These issues, though, are open to reexamination and may receive renewed attention from the Supreme Court with the additions of Chief Justice John Roberts and Justice Samuel Alito.

In the bigger picture, the establishment clause marks one of the most innovative aspects of the U.S. Constitution; the conscious decision to create separation between church and state was revolutionary at the time, and [it] continues to make the U.S. constitutional experience distinctive. That separation—which widens and narrows depending on the historical era—has created tremendous room for a vast array of religious entities to thrive. When combined with the Constitution's ban on religious test oaths (Article VI), the absolute right to believe whatever one chooses, and the principle that the government may not be co-opted by any one religion and vice versa, religious liberty and religious vitality have become a hallmark of American culture.

| "While the First Amendment keeps government out of religion, it also protects against the flip side: the injection of religion into government."

The First Amendment Provides Both Freedom of and Freedom from Religion

Jack Feerick

In the following viewpoint Jack Feerick recounts the history of the First Amendment's stance on religion. Feerick claims that despite the fact that the Founding Fathers were overwhelmingly of the same faith, the United States was founded with an eye toward religious liberty. The First Amendment of the Bill of Rights, he says, addresses this issue specifically by guaranteeing both freedom from religion and freedom of religion. Feerick claims that although the United States has always been dominantly Protestant, there is a remarkable amount of religious diversity. He concludes that the balance between religious liberty and freedom from state religion continues today to evolve through court decisions and government acts. Feerick is a writer.

Jack Feerick, "Faith in America," *Saturday Evening Post*, vol. 281, November–December 2009, p. 44. Reproduced by permission.

Thomas Jefferson didn't mince words when he gave his view on religious freedom: "It does me no injury for my neighbor to say there are twenty gods or no God," he once wrote. "It neither picks my pocket nor breaks my leg."

The First Amendment

Jefferson's no-skin-off-my-nose attitude is so thoroughly modern that it's hard to remember just how radical his view was in its day. Despite the fact that America was colonized partly by settlers looking to practice their beliefs without discrimination, the Founders still lived in a world where government-sanctioned and [government-]supported religion was the norm, where differences of faith and conscience could lead to seizure of property, bodily harm, and worse. By guaranteeing freedom of worship as a basic Constitutional right for all Americans, Jefferson and the rest of the Framers were attempting something entirely new. Almost miraculous, in fact.

Consider that the Constitution and the Bill of Rights were written and ratified by a group composed exclusively of white, male landowners (many of them slave owners), most with ties to just one specific religion—more than 50 percent of the Founding Fathers were affiliated with the Episcopal church, according to some historians. Not exactly the diverse dream team you or I might have chosen to safeguard the religious freedom of a new nation.

But that's exactly what they did, and in the first lines of the First Amendment: "Congress shall make no law respecting an establishment of religion, or prohibiting the free exercise thereof. . . ." Known forever after as the Establishment Clause, this pronouncement—and the entire amendment—has over time proven to be a versatile tool that does more than separate church and state. It protects America's faithful and faithless alike, providing both freedom of religion and freedom from it, as appropriate.

To be sure, the Founding Fathers couldn't foresee how their efforts would one day help to make America the most religiously diverse nation in the world, nor anticipate how the Establishment Clause would come into play on future issues, from the teaching of evolutionary theory in schools, to the displaying of the Ten Commandments in public buildings, to the constitutionality of the Pledge of Allegiance.

For more than 200 years, the balance between religious liberty and the rule of law has been constantly renegotiated. To understand how that balance has been maintained both then and now, we need to look back at the influences that shaped the Founders and the documents they created to serve their country and—ultimately—us.

The Faith of the Founding Fathers

The traditional idea of the Founding Fathers as conventionally pious Christian gentlemen is a myth, of course. But neither were they actively hostile to religion. John Adams, to pick one, remained a regular churchgoer throughout his long life. Jefferson, meanwhile, was skeptical of religion, yet revered Jesus as a great moral philosopher, even [going so far as to assemble] a personal edition of the New Testament with scissors and a glue-pot, retaining the ethical teachings of Christ while editing out the miracles. (You can see the Jefferson Bible today at the Smithsonian in Washington, D.C.)

The time was ripe for change. This was the Age of Enlightenment, when advances in the sciences forced philosophers to reconsider humanity's place in the universe. Educated men of the day, including Jefferson and other Founding Fathers, were attracted to Enlightenment ideals and beliefs, including Deism: the notion of a Creator whose existence could be deduced from His handiwork, but who took no active part in human affairs— God as absentee landlord.

Another Enlightenment ideal that exerted a powerful influence over the Framers was the social contract. "Social contract theory holds that government doesn't descend from on high, but from voluntary agreements among ordinary citizens," says

Gary Kowalski, author of *Revolutionary Spirits*, an account of the philosophical foundations of the Constitution. This all but flew in the face of conventional wisdom, which held that government derived its authority from God, from the top down.

As if that wasn't enough to lay the ground for revolutionary change, there was also an upswell of religious devotion among the colonial populace, with Evangelicals preaching that all men are created equal, and that each person's value is determined not by social class, but by moral behavior. Sound familiar?

The Declaration and Constitution

The Declaration of Independence, then, served not just as the founding document of the American Revolution, but as a balance of the influences of the Founders and the average citizen. It asserted our inalienable rights, endowed by our Creator. But this truth was not handed down in a mystical vision; rather it was self-evident, revealed by rational observation.

The declaration makes no further mention of God. The Founders strove to emphasize that separation from England was an expression of human rights, rather than Divine Right. "The Founders believed that religion could be a healthy force in society—if it were exercised within a zone of personal autonomy," says Kowalski.

There were practical reasons, too. Different Christian sects held majorities in different colonies—some as established churches, with taxpayer support—and religious language that appeared to favor one faith over another might have jeopardized the early union entirely. "In some respects, we bungled into religious liberty," says Charles Haynes, senior scholar at the First Amendment Center and author of several books on religion in public life. "Early on, the religious divisions in the colonies gave us little choice. So, in a way, we have religious diversity to thank for religious liberty."

Like the declaration before it, the Constitution is also relatively free of religious-speak. It does not solicit God's blessing;

instead, it begins with an invocation of "We, the People." Indeed, the Constitution's only mention of religion is negative—in Article Six, where it expressly commands that "no religious test shall ever be required as a qualification to any office or public trust under the United States."

"The lack of God-language in the Constitution is not an oversight," Kowalski says. "It provoked protest among more orthodox Christians, who thought that government needed some divine sanction." But in the end, a majority voted to keep the Constitution faith-neutral. Meanwhile, some signatories felt that the Constitution did not go far enough to guarantee basic human rights. In response, James Madison proposed a number of amendments; of the ten that comprise the Bill of Rights, the First demarcates our religious freedoms in the plain language of the Establishment Clause which, incidentally, only applies to the federal government. Several states still had established churches, while others prided themselves as havens of conscience. The Establishment Clause split the difference by throwing the issue back to the states. Those with established churches could continue to favor them, while disestablished states were free to remain so.

The true vindication for the Establishment Clause came over the years, as a sense of common American identity began to grow, and states with official churches began, one by one, to disestablish them by acts of legislature.

Diversity of Religion in America

Since its beginnings, America has been extraordinarily religiously diverse. Although it's true that, as of 1800, the majority of white Americans were Protestants of some kind, that formulation misrepresents the religious landscape of the time and the strained, even hostile relations between various congregations. The American Protestant identity—the tendency of many mainline denominations to downplay their differences and to think of themselves as "Protestant" first and foremost—only developed as immigration and expansion allowed for growth among minority faith groups. The years 1800–1850 saw U.S. population quadruple as Catholics, Lutherans, and Jews arrived from Europe, and as the country acquired territories from France, Spain, and Mexico, making their inhabitants—mostly Catholics—into newly minted U.S. citizens.

Today, as then, the country is experiencing a boom in immigration; and again, immigrants are bringing their faiths with them. Islam is considered to be one of the fastest growing religions in America. According to at least one survey, there are more

Two students pass each other at the Islamic Al Noor School in Brooklyn. The United States has always been a religiously diverse country, and Islam is one of its fastest growing religions. © AP Images/Kathy Willens.

Buddhists in America now than Evangelical Episcopalians. Some projections indicate that by mid-century, Protestant Americans will be the ones in the minority, a notion that makes many anxious, even now.

Over our country's history, different groups have been singled out as threats to national unity. In the 1800s, Catholics were the bogeyman of choice. Anti-papist preachers warned that we were losing our country to those who did not share American values. Catholics, they claimed, could never be real Americans; they owed their true allegiance to a foreign tyrant and alien laws, and were too superstitious and backward to ever blend into our society.

If that rhetoric has a familiar ring to it, it's because those same words have been used recently against other immigrant religious groups, particularly Muslims in the wake of the terrorist attacks of September 11, 2001. "Every time we come to a period in our history when we are traumatized, when we are afraid, this anxiety returns us to the idea of recovering the America that's been lost," says Haynes. But Catholics managed to assimilate within a generation or two, and the American Catholic Church proved to be a different sort of institution than the European church, simply because of the cultural and political conditions on the ground. Just so, there's reason to believe that Islam in our democratic, pluralistic society will be unlike Islam practiced elsewhere.

Religion and Law

In the 19th century, new denominations founded in the United States would prove vital to the cause of religious freedom—both for their minority status and for doctrines that brought them into conflict with the legal system.

In 1879 the Supreme Court ruled that civil laws trumped the Mormon doctrine of polygamy as a religious duty. Nasty lawsuits and countersuits raged for years, threatening the continued existence of the church itself. In the end, American identity proved so important to the Mormon church that it officially revised its religious doctrine to bring it in line with U.S. law.

But there have been times, too, when the law favored the dictates of religious conscience. In 1943 the Supreme Court reversed a ruling that originally upheld a Pennsylvania school board's expulsion of Jehovah's Witness schoolchildren who refused to salute the flag, but not before the controversy touched off a firestorm in communities across the country, where Witnesses were beaten, run out of town, or even jailed for sedition.

In recent years, the Mormon Church has cast itself as a defender of traditional marriage laws, leading the opposition to marriage rights for gays and lesbians. And by their very unwillingness to engage in secular politics, Jehovah's Witnesses have done the nation a great service in helping strengthen the protection of religious practice from government intrusion.

The Government and Religion

While the First Amendment keeps government out of religion, it also protects against the flip side: the injection of religion into government, [that is,] using the political process to pursue essentially moral goals. To be sure, many of our great social movements—abolitionism, temperance, women's rights—had religious foundations, beginning with the idea of inalienable, God-given rights. But in trying to reform American society, some movements misstepped, promoting a particular, and even particularly extreme, religious viewpoint under government auspices. Prohibition, for instance, was enacted in 1920 under pressure from a movement led by Protestant sects. Many of the measure's opponents were also people of faith, who believed that government shouldn't meddle in moral issues.

We'll probably never see Prohibition return; but other battles keep flaring up. In 2004 atheists challenged the recitation of the Pledge of Allegiance in public schools as an unconstitutional endorsement of religion because it contained the words "under God." (The motto "In God We Trust" on U.S. currency has recently come under fire for the same reason.) The Scopes trial of 1925 challenged a Tennessee law banning instruction in evolutionary theory. Eighty years later, the Kansas Board of Education voted to return creationism—calling it "Intelligent Design"—to the classroom. (The vote was reversed in 2007.)

Today, many Americans are confused and angered about the principle of separation, Haynes says. "For people afraid of losing our identity, it only pushes them to be more hostile to the First Amendment. That's dangerous because that principle is the core condition for religious freedom that protects the rights of all."

Proper understanding was just one of the areas addressed at a recent conference on the future of religious freedom in America, cosponsored by the First Amendment Center. There, policy experts identified several concerns for the future, including the consensus that free exercise of religion needs more protection still—especially for minority faiths; ways to prevent future backlash against certain religious groups—especially Muslim Americans in the wake of 9/11; and the need to provide more First Amendment education.

"The challenge is to reaffirm our commitment to religious freedom in a way that allows us to address our differences," says Haynes. "It will take a real engagement, as individuals and communities, to find a way to protect the rights of people of all faiths and no faith. I think we can do it, but we can't do it just by hoping for it."

Or praying for it.

> *"The classroom has become one of the most important battlegrounds in the broader conflict over religion's role in public life."*

Public Schools Have Long Been a Battlefield for Freedom of Religion

Ira C. Lupu, David Masci, and Robert W. Tuttle

In the following viewpoint Ira C. Lupu, David Masci, and Robert W. Tuttle claim that the battle over religion in public schools is one that began over a century ago and continues today, with the general public divided in opinion about the many issues. They cite court decisions on such issues as school prayer, the Pledge of Allegiance, graduation speeches, Bible study, and multiculturalism to illustrate how the legal understanding of the First Amendment as it applies to public schools has evolved over time. Ira C. Lupu is F. Elwood and Eleanor Davis Professor of Law at George Washington University Law School; David Masci is Senior Research Fellow at the Pew Forum on Religion & Public Life; and Robert W. Tuttle is David R. and Sherry Kirschner Berz Research Professor of Law and Religion at George Washington University Law School.

Ira C. Lupu, David Masci, and Robert W. Tuttle, "Religion in the Public Schools," The Pew Forum on Religion & Public Life, May 2007. Reproduced by permission.

Nearly a half-century after the Supreme Court issued its landmark ruling striking down school-sponsored prayer, Americans continue to fight over the place of religion in public schools. Indeed, the classroom has become one of the most important battlegrounds in the broader conflict over religion's role in public life.

Conflicts Over Religion in School

Some Americans are troubled by what they see as an effort on the part of federal courts and civil liberties advocates to exclude God and religious sentiment from public schools. Such an effort, these Americans believe, infringes upon the First Amendment right to the free exercise of religion.

Civil libertarians and others, meanwhile, voice concern that conservative Christians are trying to impose their values on students of all religious stripes. Federal courts, the civil libertarians point out, have consistently interpreted the First Amendment's prohibition on the establishment of religion to forbid state sponsorship of prayer and most other religious activities in public schools.

Despite that long series of court decisions, polls show that large numbers of Americans favor looser, not tighter, limits on religion in public schools. According to an August 2006 survey by the Pew Research Center, more than two thirds of Americans (69%) agree with the notion that "liberals have gone too far in trying to keep religion out of the schools and the government." And a clear majority (58%) favor teaching biblical creationism along with evolution in public schools.

Conflicts over religion in school are hardly new. In the 19th century, Protestants and Catholics frequently fought over Bible reading and prayer in public schools. The disputes then were over *which* Bible and *which* prayers were appropriate to use in the classroom. Some Catholics were troubled that the schools' reading materials included the King James version of the Bible, which was favored by Protestants. In 1844, fighting broke out between Protestants and Catholics in Philadelphia; a number of people died in the violence and several Catholic churches were burned. Similar conflicts erupted during the 1850s in Boston and other parts of New England. In the early 20th century, liberal Protestants and their secular allies battled religious conservatives over whether students in biology classes should be taught Charles Darwin's theory of evolution.

The Court's Interpretation

The Supreme Court stepped into those controversies when it determined, in *Cantwell v. Connecticut* (1940) and *Everson v. Board of Education of Ewing Township* (1947), that the First Amendment's Free Exercise Clause and Establishment Clause applied to the states. The two clauses say, "Congress shall make no law respecting an establishment of religion, or prohibiting the free exercise thereof." Before those two court decisions, courts had applied the religion clauses only to actions of the federal government.

Soon after the *Everson* decision, the Supreme Court began specifically applying the religion clauses to activities in public schools. In its first such case, *McCollum v. Board of Education* (1948), the high court invalidated the practice of having religious instructors from different denominations enter public schools to offer religious lessons during the school day to students whose parents requested them. A key factor in the court's decision was that the lessons took place in the schools. Four years later, in *Zorach v. Clauson*, the court upheld an arrangement by which public schools excused students during the school day so they could attend religious classes away from school property.

Beginning in the 1960s, the court handed religious conservatives a series of major defeats. It began with the landmark 1962 ruling, in *Engel v. Vitale*, that school-sponsored prayer, even if it were nonsectarian, violated the Establishment Clause. Since then, the Supreme Court has pushed forward, from banning organized

RELIGION AND POLITICS: OPINIONS IN 2006

Have liberals gone too far in trying to keep religion out of schools and government?

Yes	69%
No	26%
Don't Know	5%
	100%

Have conservatives gone too far in trying to impose their religious values on the country?

Yes	49%
No	43%
Don't Know	8%
	100%

The Republican Party's attitude toward religion is...

Friendly	47%
Neutral	28%
Unfriendly	13%
Don't Know	12%
	100%

The Democratic Party's attitude toward religion is...

Friendly	26%
Neutral	42%
Unfriendly	20%
Don't Know	12%
	100%

Taken from: "Many Americans Uneasy with Mix of Religion and Politics," Pew Forum on Religion & Public Life, August 2006.

Bible reading for religious and moral instruction in 1963 to prohibiting prayers at high school football games in 2000.

In these and other decisions, the court has repeatedly stressed that the Constitution prohibits public schools from indoctrinating children in religion. But it is not always easy to determine exactly what constitutes indoctrination or school sponsorship of religious activities. For example, can a class on the Bible as literature be taught without a bias for or against the idea that the Bible is religious truth? Can students be compelled to participate in a Christmas-themed music program? Sometimes students themselves, rather than teachers, administrators or coaches, bring their faith into school activities. For instance, when a student invokes gratitude to God in a valedictory address, or a high school football player offers a prayer in a huddle, is the school legally responsible for their religious expression? . . .

The Issue of School Prayer

The most enduring and controversial issue related to school-sponsored religious activities is classroom prayer. In *Engel v. Vitale* . . . the Supreme Court held that the Establishment Clause prohibited the recitation of a school-sponsored prayer in public schools. *Engel* involved a simple and seemingly nonsectarian prayer composed especially for use in New York's public schools. In banning the prayer exercise entirely, the court did not rest its opinion on the grounds that unwilling students were coerced to pray; that would come much later. Rather, the court emphasized what it saw as the wrongs of having the government create and sponsor a religious activity.

The following year, the high court extended the principle outlined in *Engel* to a program of daily Bible reading. In *Abington School District v. Schempp*, the court ruled broadly that school sponsorship of religious exercises violates the Constitution. *Schempp* became the source of the enduring constitutional doctrine that all government action must have a predominantly secular purpose—a requirement that, according to the court, the

Bible-reading exercise clearly could not satisfy. By insisting that religious expression be excluded from the formal curriculum, the Supreme Court was assuring parents that public schools would be officially secular and would not compete with parents in their children's religious upbringing.

With *Engel* and *Schempp*, the court outlined the constitutional standard for prohibiting school-sponsored religious expression, a doctrine the court has firmly maintained. In *Stone v. Graham* (1980), for instance, it found unconstitutional a Kentucky law requiring all public schools to post a copy of the Ten Commandments. And in *Wallace v. Jaffree* (1985), it overturned an Alabama law requiring public schools to set aside a moment each day for silent prayer or meditation.

School sponsorship of student-led prayer has fared no better. In 2000, the Supreme Court ruled in *Santa Fe Independent School District v. Doe* that schools may not sponsor student-recited prayer at high school football games.

More sweeping in its consequences is *Lee v. Weisman* (1992), which invalidated a school-sponsored prayer led by an invited clergyman at a public school commencement in Providence, [Rhode Island]. The court's 5–4 decision rested explicitly on the argument that graduating students were being forced to participate in a religious ceremony. The case effectively outlawed a practice that was customary in many communities across the country, thus fueling the conservative critique that the Supreme Court was inhospitable to public expressions of faith.

So far, lower appellate courts have not extended the principles of the school prayer decisions to university commencements. The 4th Circuit, however, found unconstitutional the practice of daily prayer at supper at the Virginia Military Institute. In that case, *Mellen v. Bunting* (2003), the appellate court reasoned that VMI's military-like environment tended to coerce participation by cadets. The decision was similar to an earlier ruling by the U.S. Circuit Court of Appeals for the District of Columbia, which found unconstitutional a policy of the U.S. service academies that all cadets and midshipmen attend Protestant, Catholic or Jewish chapel services on Sunday. For the court, the key element was the service academies' coercion of students to attend the religious activity.

The Pledge of Allegiance

In 1954, Congress revised the Pledge of Allegiance to refer to the nation as "under God," a phrase that has since been recited by generations of schoolchildren. In 2000, Michael Newdow filed suit challenging the phrase on behalf of his daughter, a public school student in California. Newdow argued that the words "under God" violated the Establishment Clause because they transformed the pledge into a religious exercise.

The case, *Elk Grove Unified School District v. Newdow*, reached the Supreme Court in 2004, but the justices did not ultimately decide whether the phrase was acceptable. Instead, the court ruled that Newdow lacked standing to bring the suit because he did not have legal custody of his daughter. In concurring opinions, however, four justices expressed the view that the Constitution permitted recitation of the pledge—with the phrase "under God"—in public schools.

Since then, the issue has not again reached the Supreme Court but is still being litigated in the lower courts. In *Myers v. Loudoun County Public Schools* (2005), the 4th U.S. Circuit Court of Appeals upheld the reciting of the pledge in Virginia, but a U.S. district court in California ruled the other way in a new suit involving Michael Newdow and other parents. The court ruling in California, *Newdow v. Congress of the United States* (2005), is on appeal in the 9th U.S. Circuit Court of Appeals [in 2010 the Court rejected the claim that "under God" violated the First Amendment].

School Officials and Student Speech

The courts have drawn a sharp distinction between officially sponsored religious speech, such as a benediction by an invited clergyman at a commencement ceremony, and private religious speech by students. The Supreme Court made clear in *Lee v. Weisman* . . . that a clergyman's benediction at a public school event would violate the separation of church and state. Judges usually reach that same conclusion when school officials cooperate with students to produce student-delivered religious messages. But federal courts are more divided in cases involving students acting on their own to include a religious sentiment or prayer at a school commencement or a similar activity.

Some courts, particularly in the South, have upheld the constitutionality of student-initiated religious speech, emphasizing the private origins of this kind of religious expression. As long as school officials did not encourage or explicitly approve the contents, those courts have upheld religious content in student commencement speeches.

In *Adler v. Duval County School Board* (1996), for example, the 11th U.S. Circuit Court of Appeals approved a system at a Florida high school in which the senior class, acting independently of school officials, selected a class member to deliver a commencement address. School officials neither influenced the choice of speaker nor screened the speech. Under those circumstances, the appeals court ruled that the school was not responsible for the religious content of the address.

Other courts, however, have invalidated school policies that permit student speakers to include religious sentiments in graduation addresses. One leading case is *ACLU v. Black Horse Pike Regional Board of Education* (1996), in which the senior class of a New Jersey public high school selected the student speaker by a vote without knowing in advance the contents of the student's remarks. The 3rd U.S. Circuit Court of Appeals nevertheless ruled that the high school could not permit religious content in the commencement speech. The court reasoned that students attending the graduation ceremony were as coerced to acquiesce in a student-led prayer as they would be if the prayer were offered by a member of the clergy, the practice forbidden by *Weisman* in 1992. (Supreme Court Justice Samuel Alito, who was then a member of the appeals court, joined a dissenting opinion in the case, arguing that the graduating students' rights to religious and expressive freedom should prevail over the Establishment Clause concerns.)

Similarly, in *Bannon v. School District of Palm Beach County* (2004), the 11th U.S. Circuit Court of Appeals ruled that Florida school officials were right to order the removal of student-created religious messages and symbols from a school beautification project. The court reasoned that the project was not intended as a forum for the expression of students' private views but rather as a school activity for which school officials would be held responsible.

Religion in the Curriculum

The Supreme Court's decisions about officially sponsored religious expression in schools consistently draw a distinction between religious activities such as worship or Bible reading, which are designed to inculcate religious sentiments and values, and "teaching about religion," which is both constitutionally permissible and educationally appropriate. On several occasions, members of the court have suggested that public schools may teach "the Bible as literature," include lessons about the role of religion and religious institutions in history, or offer courses on comparative religion. . . .

Courts have also expended significant time and energy considering public school programs involving Bible study. Although the Supreme Court has occasionally referred to the permissibility of teaching the Bible as literature, some school districts have instituted Bible study programs that courts have found unconstitutional. Frequently, judges have concluded that these courses are thinly disguised efforts to teach a particular understanding of the New Testament.

In a number of these cases, school districts have brought in outside groups to run the Bible study program. The groups, in turn, hired their own teachers, in some cases Bible college students or members of the clergy who did not meet state accreditation standards.

Such Bible study programs have generally been held unconstitutional because, the courts conclude, they teach the Bible as religious truth or are designed to inculcate particular religious sentiments. For a public school class to study the Bible without violating constitutional limits, the class would have to include critical rather than devotional readings and allow open inquiry into the history and content of biblical passages.

Holiday Programs and Multiculturalism

Christmas themed music programs also have raised constitutional concerns. For a holiday music program to be constitutionally sound, the courts maintain, school officials must ensure the predominance of secular considerations, such as the program's educational value or the musical qualities of the pieces. The schools also must be sensitive to the possibility that some students will feel coerced to participate in the program. Moreover, the courts have said, no student should be forced to sing or play music that offends his religious sensibilities. Therefore, schools must allow students to choose not to participate.

Not all the cases involving religion in the curriculum concern the promotion of the beliefs of the majority. In a number of recent cases, challenges have come from Christian groups arguing that school policies discriminate against Christianity by promoting cultural pluralism.

In a recent example, the 2nd U.S. Circuit Court of Appeals considered a New York City Department of Education policy regulating the types of symbols displayed during the holiday seasons of various religions. The department allows the display of a menorah as a symbol of Hanukkah and a star and crescent as a symbol of Ramadan but permits the display of only secular symbols of Christmas, such as a Christmas tree; it explicitly

Michael Newdow walked past protesters in 2004 as he challenged the constitutionality of the phrase "under God" in the Pledge of Allegiance. © Mannie Garcia/Getty Images.

forbids the display of a Christmas nativity scene in public schools.

Upholding the city's policy, the Court of Appeals reasoned in *Skoros v. Klein* (2006) that city officials intended to promote cultural pluralism in the highly diverse setting of the New York City public schools. The court concluded that a "reasonable observer" would understand that the menorah and star/crescent combination had secular as well as religious meanings. The judicial panel ruled that the policy, therefore, did not promote Judaism or Islam and did not denigrate Christianity.

In another high-profile case, *Citizens for a Responsible Curriculum v. Montgomery County Public Schools* (2005), a Maryland citizens' group successfully challenged a health education curriculum that included discussion of sexual orientation. Ordinarily, opponents of homosexuality could not confidently cite the Establishment Clause as the basis for a complaint, because the curriculum typically would not advance a particular religious perspective. However, the Montgomery County curriculum included materials in teacher guides that disparaged some religious teachings on homosexuality as theologically flawed, and contrasted those teachings with what the guide portrayed as the more acceptable and tolerant views of some other faiths. The district court concluded that the curriculum had both the purpose and effect of advancing certain faiths while denigrating the beliefs of others. The county has now rewritten these materials to exclude any reference to the views of particular faiths. These new materials will be more difficult to challenge successfully in court because the lessons do not condemn or praise any faith tradition.

> *"It is no part of the business of government to compose official prayers for any group of the American people to recite as a part of a religious program."*

It Is a Violation of the First Amendment to Require Prayer in Public Schools

The Supreme Court's Decision

Hugo Black

In the following viewpoint Justice Hugo Black, writing for the majority of the Court, argues that a New York law requiring school-children to join in a daily prayer is unconstitutional. The Court contends that the Establishment Clause of the First Amendment to the US Constitution prohibits the government from promoting any religious beliefs through school prayer. Furthermore, the Court claims that even if school-mandated prayer is nondenominational or students are given the option to participate, such government promotion of religion is a violation of the First Amendment. The decision in Engel v. Vitale *(1962) became the basis for several subsequent school-prayer decisions in following years. Black was associate justice of the US Supreme Court from 1937 until his retirement in 1971.*

The respondent Board of Education of Union Free School District No. 9, New Hyde Park, New York, acting in its official capacity under State law, directed the School District's principal to cause the following prayer to be said aloud by each class in the presence of a teacher at the beginning of each school day:

> Almighty God, we acknowledge our dependence upon Thee, and we beg Thy blessings upon us, our parents, our teachers and our Country.

This daily procedure was adopted on the recommendation of the State Board of Regents, a governmental agency created by the State Constitution to which the New York Legislature has granted broad supervisory, executive, and legislative powers over the State's public school system. These State officials composed the prayer, which they recommended and published as a part of their "Statement on Moral and Spiritual Training in the Schools," saying:

> We believe that this Statement will be subscribed to by all men and women of good will, and we call upon all of them to aid in giving life to our program.

An Objection to School Prayer

Shortly after the practice of reciting the Regents' prayer was adopted by the School District, the parents of ten pupils brought this action in a New York State Court, insisting that use of this official prayer in the public schools was contrary to the beliefs, religions, or religious practices of both themselves and their children. Among other things, these parents challenged the constitutionality of both the State law authorizing the School District to direct the use of prayer in public schools and the School District's regulation ordering the recitation of this particular prayer on the ground that these actions of official governmental agencies violate that part of the First Amendment of the Federal Constitution which commands that "Congress shall make no law respecting an establishment of religion"—a command which was "made applicable to the State of New York by the Fourteenth Amendment of the said Constitution." . . .

We think that, by using its public school system to encourage recitation of the Regents' prayer, the State of New York has adopted a practice wholly inconsistent with the Establishment Clause. There can, of course, be no doubt that New York's program of daily classroom invocation of God's blessings as prescribed in the Regents' prayer is a religious activity. It is a solemn avowal of divine faith and supplication for the blessings of the Almighty. The nature of such a prayer has always been religious, none of the respondents has denied this, and the trial court expressly so found:

> The religious nature of prayer was recognized by Jefferson, and has been concurred in by theological writers, the United States Supreme Court, and State courts and administrative officials, including New York's Commissioner of Education. A committee of the New York Legislature has agreed.
>
> The Board of Regents as *amicus curiae* [friend of the court], the respondents, and interveners all concede the religious nature of prayer, but seek to distinguish this prayer because it is based on our spiritual heritage. . . .

The petitioners contend, among other things, that the State laws requiring or permitting use of the Regents' prayer must be struck down as a violation of the Establishment Clause because that prayer was composed by governmental officials as a part of a governmental program to further religious beliefs. For this reason, petitioners argue, the State's use of the Regents' prayer in its public school system breaches the constitutional wall of separation between Church and State. We agree with that contention, since we think that the constitutional prohibition against laws respecting an establishment of religion must at least mean that, in this country, it is no part of the business of government to compose official prayers for any group of the American people to recite as a part of a religious program carried on by government. . . .

The Government and Religion

There can be no doubt that New York's State prayer program officially establishes the religious beliefs embodied in the Regents' prayer. The respondents' argument to the contrary, which is largely based upon the contention that the Regents' prayer is "nondenominational" and the fact that the program, as modified and approved by State courts, does not require all pupils to recite the prayer, but permits those who wish to do so to remain silent or be excused from the room, ignores the essential nature of the

Some of the parents who brought suit against the New York public schools in 1962 due to the district's enforcement of prayer in the classroom sit with their children. Thelma Engel sits middle row, far left. © AP Images.

program's constitutional defects. Neither the fact that the prayer may be denominationally neutral nor the fact that its observance on the part of the students is voluntary can serve to free it from the limitations of the Establishment Clause, as it might from the Free Exercise Clause, of the First Amendment, both of which are operative against the States by virtue of the Fourteenth Amendment. Although these two clauses may, in certain instances, overlap, they forbid two quite different kinds of governmental encroachment upon religious freedom. The Establishment Clause, unlike the Free Exercise Clause, does not depend upon any showing of direct governmental compulsion and is violated by the enactment of laws which establish an official religion whether those laws operate directly to coerce nonobserving individuals or not. This is not to say, of course, that laws officially prescribing a particular form of religious worship do not involve coercion of such individuals. When the power, prestige, and financial support of government [are] placed behind a particular religious belief, the indirect coercive pressure upon religious minorities to conform to the prevailing officially approved religion is plain. But the purposes underlying the Establishment Clause go much further than that. Its first and most immediate purpose rested on the belief that a union of government and religion tends to destroy government and to degrade religion. The history of governmentally established religion, both in England and in this country, showed that whenever government had allied itself with one particular form of religion, the inevitable result had been that it had incurred the hatred, disrespect, and even contempt of those who held contrary beliefs. That same history showed that many people had lost their respect for any religion that had relied upon the support of government to spread its faith. The Establishment Clause thus stands as an expression of principle on the part of the Founders of our Constitution that religion is too personal, too sacred, too holy, to permit its "unhallowed perversion" by a civil magistrate. Another purpose of the Establishment Clause rested upon an awareness of the historical fact that governmen-

TEEN SUPPORT FOR SCHOOL PRAYER

Please indicate whether or not each of the following should be allowed in public schools:

■ Yes   □ No

A spoken prayer that specifically mentions Jesus Christ

44%

56%

A spoken prayer that does not mention any specific religion

58%

42%

A moment of silence to allow students to pray if they want to

84%

16%

Asked of U.S. teens aged 13–17

Taken from: Gallup Poll, April 15–May 22, 2005.

tally established religions and religious persecutions go hand in hand. The Founders knew that, only a few years after the Book of Common Prayer became the only accepted form of religious services in the established Church of England, an Act of Uniformity was passed to compel all Englishmen to attend those services and to make it a criminal offense to conduct or attend religious gatherings of any other kind—a law which was consistently flouted by dissenting religious groups in England and which contributed to widespread persecutions of people like John Bunyan, who persisted in holding "unlawful [religious] meetings . . . to the great disturbance and distraction of the good subjects of this kingdom. . . ." And they knew that similar persecutions had received the sanction of law in several of the colonies in this country soon after the establishment of official religions in those colonies. It was in large part to get completely away from this sort of systematic religious persecution that the Founders brought into being our Nation, our Constitution, and our Bill of Rights, with its prohibition against any governmental establishment of religion. The New York laws officially prescribing the Regents' prayer are inconsistent both with the purposes of the Establishment Clause and with the Establishment Clause itself.

It has been argued that to apply the Constitution in such a way as to prohibit State laws respecting an establishment of religious services in public schools is to indicate a hostility toward religion or toward prayer. Nothing, of course, could be more wrong. The history of man is inseparable from the history of religion. And perhaps it is not too much to say that, since the beginning of that history, many people have devoutly believed that "More things are wrought by prayer than this world dreams of." It was doubtless largely due to men who believed this that there grew up a sentiment that caused men to leave the cross-currents of officially established State religions and religious persecution in Europe and come to this country filled with the hope that they could find a place in which they could pray when they pleased to the God of their faith in the language they chose. And there were men of this same faith in the power of prayer who led the fight for adoption of our Constitution and also for our Bill of Rights with the very guarantees of religious freedom that forbid the sort of governmental activity which New York has attempted here. These men knew that the First Amendment, which tried to put an end to governmental control of religion and of prayer, was not written to destroy either. They knew, rather, that it was written to quiet well justified fears which nearly all of them felt arising out of an awareness that governments of the past had shackled men's tongues to make them speak only the religious thoughts that government wanted them to speak and to pray only to the God that government wanted them to pray to. It is neither sacrilegious nor anti-religious to say that each separate government in this country should stay out of the business of writing or sanctioning official prayers and leave that purely religious function to the people themselves and to those the people choose to look to for religious guidance.

> *"The laws require religious exercises,*
> *and such exercises are being conducted*
> *in direct violation of the rights of the*
> *appellees and petitioners."*

It Is Unconstitutional for Public Schools to Read Passages of the Bible

The Supreme Court's Decision

Tom C. Clark

In the following viewpoint Justice Tom C. Clark, writing for the majority of the Court, contends that two different state laws requiring Bible passages to be read in public school are in violation of the Establishment Clause of the First Amendment, which prevents government from advancing any particular religion. The Court argues that requiring passages of the Bible to be read, even if for an alleged nonreligious purpose such as teaching morality, constitutes a religious exercise. Furthermore, though the Court notes that the Free Exercise Clause of the First Amendment prevents the government from interfering with any individual's free exercise of his or her religion, the Court denies that the majority may decide to implement religious practices in public school without a violation of the establishment clause. Clark was associate justice of the US Supreme Court from 1949 until his retirement in 1967.

Tom C. Clark, Majority opinion, *Abington Township v. Schempp*, US Supreme Court, June 17, 1963. Copyright © 1963 The Supreme Court of the United States.

Once again, we are called upon to consider the scope of the provision of the First Amendment to the United States Constitution which declares that "Congress shall make no law respecting an establishment of religion, or prohibiting the free exercise thereof. . . ." These companion cases present the issues in the context of state action requiring that schools begin each day with readings from the Bible. While raising the basic questions under slightly different factual situations, the cases permit of joint treatment. In light of the history of the First Amendment and of our cases interpreting and applying its requirements, we hold that the practices at issue and the laws requiring them are unconstitutional under the Establishment Clause, as applied to the States through the Fourteenth Amendment.

The Schempp Family in Pennsylvania

The Facts in Each Case: No. 142. The Commonwealth of Pennsylvania, by law . . . requires that

> At least ten verses from the Holy Bible shall be read, without comment, at the opening of each public school on each school day. Any child shall be excused from such Bible reading, or attending such Bible reading, upon the written request of his parent or guardian.

The Schempp family, husband and wife and two of their three children, brought suit to enjoin enforcement of the statute, contending that their rights under the Fourteenth Amendment to the Constitution of the United States are, have been, and will continue to be, violated unless this statute be declared unconstitutional as violative of these provisions of the First Amendment. They sought to enjoin the appellant school district, wherein the Schempp children attend school, and its officers and the Superintendent of Public Instruction of the Commonwealth from continuing to conduct such readings and recitation of the Lord's Prayer in the public schools of the district pursuant to the statute. . . .

The appellees Edward Lewis Schempp, his wife Sidney, and their children, Roger and Donna, are of the Unitarian faith, and are members of the Unitarian Church in Germantown, Philadelphia, Pennsylvania, where they, as well as another son, Ellory [he later changed the spelling of his name to Ellery], regularly attend religious services. The latter was originally a party, but, having graduated from the school system *pendente lite* [while the litigation was pending], was voluntarily dismissed from the action. The other children attend the Abington Senior High School, which is a public school operated by appellant district.

On each school day at the Abington Senior High School between 8:15 and 8:30 A.M., while the pupils are attending their home rooms or advisory sections, opening exercises are conducted pursuant to the statute. The exercises are broadcast into each room in the school building through an intercommunications system, and are conducted under the supervision of a teacher by students attending the school's radio and television workshop. Selected students from this course gather each morning in the school's workshop studio for the exercises, which include readings by one of the students of 10 verses of the Holy Bible, broadcast to each room in the building. This is followed by the recitation of the Lord's Prayer, likewise over the intercommunications system, but also by the students in the various classrooms, who are asked to stand and join in repeating the prayer in unison. The exercises are closed with the flag salute and such pertinent announcements as are of interest to the students. Participation in the opening exercises, as directed by the statute, is voluntary. The student reading the verses from the Bible may select the passages and read from any version he chooses, although the only copies furnished by the school are the King James version, copies of which were circulated to each teacher by the school district. During the period in which the exercises have been conducted, the King James, the Douay, and the Revised Standard versions of the Bible have been used, as well as the Jewish Holy Scriptures. There are no prefatory statements, no questions asked or solicited, no comments or explanations made, and no interpretations given at or during the exercises. The students and parents are advised that the student may absent himself from the classroom or, should he elect to remain, not participate in the exercises.

It appears from the record that, in schools not having an intercommunications system, the Bible reading and the recitation of the Lord's Prayer were conducted by the home-room teacher, who chose the text of the verses and read them herself or had students read them in rotation or by volunteers. This was followed by a standing recitation of the Lord's Prayer, together with the Pledge of Allegiance to the Flag by the class in unison and a closing announcement of routine school items of interest.

At the first trial, Edward Schempp and the children testified as to specific religious doctrines purveyed by a literal reading of the Bible "which were contrary to the religious beliefs which they held, and to their familial teaching." The children testified that all of the doctrines to which they referred were read to them at various times as part of the exercises. Edward Schempp testified at the second trial that he had considered having Roger and Donna excused from attendance at the exercises, but [he] decided against it for several reasons, including his belief that the children's relationships with their teachers and classmates would be adversely affected. . . .

The Murray Family in Maryland

No. 119. In 1905, the Board of School Commissioners of Baltimore City adopted a rule pursuant to Art. 77, § 202 of the Annotated Code of Maryland. The rule provided for the holding of opening exercises in the schools of the city, consisting primarily of the "reading, without comment, of a chapter in the Holy Bible and/or the use of the Lord's Prayer." The petitioners, Mrs. Madalyn Murray and her son, William J. Murray III, are both professed atheists. Following unsuccessful attempts to have the respondent school board rescind the rule, this suit was filed for mandamus [an order from a higher court] to compel its rescission and cancellation. It was alleged that William was a student in a public school of the city, and Mrs. Murray, his mother, was a taxpayer therein; that it was the practice under the rule to have a reading on each school morning from the King James version of the Bible; that, at petitioners' insistence, the rule was amended to permit children to be excused from the exercise on request of the parent, and that William had been excused pursuant thereto; that nevertheless the rule as amended was in violation of the petitioners' rights "to freedom of religion under the First and Fourteenth Amendments" and in violation of "the principle of separation between church and state, contained therein. . . ." The petition particularized the petitioners' atheistic beliefs and stated that the rule, as practiced, violated their rights

> in that it threatens their religious liberty by placing a premium on belief as against nonbelief and subjects their freedom of conscience to the rule of the majority; it pronounces belief in God as the source of all moral and spiritual values, equating these values with religious values, and thereby renders sinister, alien and suspect the beliefs and ideals of your Petitioners,

promoting doubt and question of their morality, good citizenship and good faith. . . .

The Establishment Clause of the First Amendment

The Establishment Clause has been directly considered by this Court eight times in the past score of years and, with only one Justice dissenting on the point, it has consistently held that the clause withdrew all legislative power respecting religious belief or the expression thereof. The test may be stated as follows: what are the purpose and the primary effect of the enactment? If either is the advancement or inhibition of religion, then the enactment exceeds the scope of legislative power as circumscribed by the Constitution. That is to say that, to withstand the strictures of the Establishment Clause, there must be a secular legislative purpose and a primary effect that neither advances nor inhibits religion. The Free Exercise Clause, likewise considered many times here, withdraws from legislative power, state and federal, the exertion of any restraint on the free exercise of religion. Its purpose is to secure religious liberty in the individual by prohibiting any invasions thereof by civil authority. Hence, it is necessary in a free exercise case for one to show the coercive effect of the enactment as it operates against him in the practice of his religion. The distinction between the two clauses is apparent—a violation of the Free Exercise Clause is predicated on coercion, while the Establishment Clause violation need not be so attended.

Applying the Establishment Clause principles to the cases at bar, we find that the States are requiring the selection and reading at the opening of the school day of verses from the Holy Bible and the recitation of the Lord's Prayer by the students in unison. These exercises are prescribed as part of the curricular activities of students who are required by law to attend school. They are held in the school buildings under the supervision and with the participation of teachers employed in those schools. . . . The trial court in No. 142 has found that such an opening exercise is a religious ceremony, and was intended by the State to be so. We agree with the trial court's finding as to the religious character of the exercises. Given that finding, the exercises and the law requiring them are in violation of the Establishment Clause.

There is no such specific finding as to the religious character of the exercises in No. 119, and the State contends (as does the State in No. 142) that the program is an effort to extend its benefits to all public school children without regard to their religious belief. Included within its secular purposes, it says, are the promotion of moral values, the contradiction to the materialistic trends of our times, the perpetuation of our institutions and the teaching of literature. The case came up on demurrer [objection]; of course, to a petition which alleged that the uniform practice under the rule had been to read from the King James version of the Bible, and that the exercise was sectarian. The short answer, therefore, is that the religious character of the exercise was admitted by the State. But even if its purpose is not strictly religious, it is sought to be accomplished through readings, without comment, from the Bible. Surely the place of the Bible as an instrument of religion cannot be gainsaid, and the State's recognition of the pervading religious character of the ceremony is evident from the rule's specific permission of the alternative use of the Catholic Douay version, as well as the recent amendment permitting nonattendance at the exercises. None of these factors is consistent with the contention that the Bible is here used either as an instrument for nonreligious moral inspiration or as a reference for the teachings of secular subjects.

A Violation of Neutrality

The conclusion follows that, in both cases, the laws require religious exercises, and such exercises are being conducted in direct violation of the rights of the appellees and petitioners. Nor are these required exercises mitigated by the fact that individual students may absent themselves upon parental request, for that fact furnishes no defense to a claim of unconstitutionality under the

Establishment Clause. Further, it is no defense to urge that the religious practices here may be relatively minor encroachments on the First Amendment. The breach of neutrality that is today a trickling stream may all too soon become a raging torrent and, in the words of [James] Madison, "it is proper to take alarm at the first experiment on our liberties."

It is insisted that, unless these religious exercises are permitted, a "religion of secularism" is established in the schools. We agree, of course, that the State may not establish a "religion of secularism" in the sense of affirmatively opposing or showing hostility to religion, thus "preferring those who believe in no religion over those who do believe" [*Zorach v. Clauson* (1952)]. We do not agree, however, that this decision in any sense has that effect. In addition, it might well be said that one's education is not complete without a study of comparative religion or the history of religion and its relationship to the advancement of civilization. It certainly may be said that the Bible is worthy of study for its literary and historic qualities. Nothing we have said here indicates that such study of the Bible or of religion, when presented objectively as part of a secular program of education, may not be effected consistently with the First Amendment. But the exercises here do not fall into those categories. They are religious exercises, required by the States in violation of the command of the First Amendment that the Government maintain strict neutrality, neither aiding nor opposing religion.

Finally, we cannot accept that the concept of neutrality, which does not permit a State to require a religious exercise even with the consent of the majority of those affected, collides with the majority's right to free exercise of religion. While the Free Exercise Clause clearly prohibits the use of state action to deny the rights of free exercise to *anyone*, it has never meant that a majority could use the machinery of the State to practice its beliefs.

| *"The role of separation of church and state is all important."*

Ellery Schempp Discusses the *Schempp* Court Case and Current Church-State Separation

Personal Narrative

David Niose

In the following viewpoint David Niose interviews Ellery Schempp, one of the original student plaintiffs in Abington Township v. Schempp *(1963), for* The Humanist *magazine. Almost half a century after the case, Schempp celebrates the Court's decision to prevent states from imposing the religious practice of Bible reading on public schoolchildren. Schempp explains his religious philosophy at the time of the case and how it has evolved. Schempp also discusses his optimism for the continued separation of church and state in the United States, though he cautions that the composition of the US Supreme Court is quite a bit different than it was when his case was heard. Niose is a Massachusetts attorney and president of the*

David Niose, "The *Humanist* Interview: Ellery Schempp," *Humanist,* vol. 68, January–February 2008, pp. 36–39. Reproduced by permission of the author.

board of directors of the American Humanist Association, a non-theistic organization.

On November 26, 1956, sixteen-year-old Ellery Schempp staged a protest against his public high school's daily Bible reading and prayer requirement by bringing a copy of the Quran to class and reading silently from it. After he was reprimanded he and his parents sued the school district. The case was taken up by the ACLU [American Civil Liberties Union] and eventually led to the landmark 1963 U.S. Supreme Court decision *Abington v. Schempp* and *Murray v. Curlett* that declared devotional Bible readings in public schools unconstitutional. Schempp went on to earn a bachelor's degree from Tufts University in physics and his Ph.D. in physics from Brown University. He has held numerous academic and research positions, including at the University of Pittsburgh, Lawrence Berkeley National Laboratory, and with the Harvard Consulting group, focusing his research in the areas of chemical physics, energy conservation, and MRI technology. Schempp is a member of the American Humanist Association [and] Americans United for Separation of Church and State, and [he] sits on the Advisory Board of the Secular Student Alliance.

Ellery's Protest: How One Young Man Defied Tradition and Sparked the Battle over School Prayer by Stephen D. Solomon was published by University of Michigan Press in August 2007. *The Humanist* caught up with Schempp shortly thereafter to discuss his protest, the philosophy behind it, and the status of church-state separation under the current Supreme Court.

The 1963 Court Case

The Humanist: Do you consider it fortunate that your case was heard by the Earl Warren court? After all, it's hard to imagine a William Rehnquist court or a John Roberts court handing down that kind of precedent.

Ellery Schempp: I think Warren and the justices at that time had a sense of community, a sense of understanding how our Constitution applies to contemporary Americans. Warren had experience as an elected governor, and had strong convictions about the Bill of Rights from a human perspective. Warren, of course, was merely one vote among nine. But justices like William Brennan, John Marshall Harlan, Arthur Goldberg, William O. Douglas, and Tom C. Clark thought about social comity. This is different from justices who are focused on catechism of law. The Roberts-Scalia-Thomas-Alito-wing comes from a reduced background, and mostly from an authoritarian bent in their approach, perhaps owing to a common hierarchical religious adherence. . . .

Stephen D. Solomon's new book, Ellery's Protest . . . *details your objection, as a high-school student, to mandatory school prayer and Bible reading that ultimately led to one of the Supreme Court's most important rulings on religious freedom. Can you describe the path that led you to take such a historic stand?*

I was very interested in the structure of the earth and the solar system from the time I was about six years old. The explanation that "God did it" distinctly didn't appeal to me, and the notion of heaven and hell—and their locations—mixed up with a god seemed particularly silly and problematic.

Attending a Unitarian Universalist church as a child, I never held any view that the Bible was literally true or that Jesus was a "son of God," and by the time I learned about the birds and bees, the notion of an immaculate conception and virgin birth seemed wildly improbable. And since the biblical account of Noah and the flood seemed nuts, I came to think the rest of it was of little "truthiness."

My protest back in 1956 had something to do with standing up for a minority and a sense of social justice. An important influence on me, and an unfortunate omission in Solomon's book was *The Democratic Way of Life: An American Interpretation* by T.V. Smith and Eduard C. Lindeman. This book gave me a sense of fraternity, liberty, and equality and of the role and rights of the minority that stirred me then. Smith and Lindeman made no mention of God, but provided stirring rhetoric for a sixteen-year-old's faith in an idealized American democracy.

Religious Philosophies
What effect did your parents' religious philosophies have on you?

My mother, Sidney, was amused by so many gods making claims that various humans took seriously, and she definitely rejected the existence of "godly demons and devils"; she consistently saw war as evil, and couldn't accept that religions could "justify" war. My father struggled with a god belief for most of his life, and he was always perplexed by how people could do the most awful things "in the name of God." He had trouble accepting that people could believe the events of Genesis, the concept of "chosen people," miracles, terrible acts of violence in Leviticus, and so forth and still be quite reasonable and decent people. (He often said that he was attracted to Unitarians because "you didn't have to park your brain at the church door.")

I adopted the view that life was holistic and not divided into separate realms; that things had to make sense in all domains. When I was in academia, I often pointed out that the real world doesn't come divided into geology, physics, and chemistry, for example; these designations are for the convenience of teachers. I did my doctoral work in the interdisciplinary field of chemical physics, and with a life-long interest in geology and a passing knowledge of biology. I have enjoyed making connections among the disciplines.

If I'm not mistaken, I read somewhere that you've only begun openly identifying as an atheist relatively recently, within the last decade or so. Is that true? What led to your decision?

In my twenties and thirties, I would say I was agnostic, but I was really developing my present view. I recall one occasion when someone really wanted an answer, and I asked, "Why is this so important to you?" My questioner clearly wanted to put everyone into boxes: "good" people, "okay" people who might be misguided or not yet informed, and "bad" people. It reminded me of my high school principal, Mr. Stuhl, who was proud to be a lay Methodist preacher and who liked identifying the "rotten apples" in the barrel.

I shied away from the word "atheist" most of my life, partly I think because of [founder of the American Atheists organization] Madalyn Murray O'Hair's stridency, perhaps because of the general opprobrium that is attached to atheists. Most of my life, I actually wanted to be accepted, loved, and appreciated as a member of society—and have jobs, perhaps being a bit colorful and independent, but surely not looking for isolation and rejection.

About a decade ago, I began to wonder why I wasn't an atheist. I knew I was a humanist, even during the many years I wasn't a member of any church, nor of the several humanist associations in existence. That is, I thought that we humans were in charge of our own destiny, and I absolutely rejected the idea that some supernatural intervention would rescue us—if we indeed needed rescuing. The human mind's capacity for imagining all sorts of things—in fiction, dreams, fears, wishful thinking—is impressive. And for those disposed to an authority figure for their lives the thing is God. Incidentally, I never understood the appeal of a single god. It must have been far simpler when we had a rain god, a fertility god, a crop god, and so forth—then we knew who we were angry at if the rain didn't come and you could rant against him without upsetting the whole of the universe. Monotheism made this more complicated. Now the god who sends hurricanes and earthquakes doesn't get blamed, but rather humans of a certain sexual orientation.

I do accept that a god-belief is very real for many people, but never having found any evidence in the natural world for gods, ghosts, gurus, astrologers, Atlanteans, homoeopathists, and the whole ocean of non-natural beliefs, I decided that I could join the community of nonbelievers and skeptics who call themselves atheists. . . .

The Separation of Church and State

How do you feel about the current state of church-state separation in the United States and the Roberts court as a defender of that separation?

The role of separation of church and state is all important—*it does government no good to rely on magical thinking, and it does religion no good to be separated from reality.* When you think about it, the Bible never once mentions democracy, a republic, or anything related to American values. The Bible never mentions freedom of speech or freedom of religion. It doesn't mention separation of powers and limitations on the power of the executive; it doesn't mention elections or religious tolerance. The Bible provides no model for "good" government or for personal freedoms. It is a purely religious/theological document.

I am optimistic about continued church-state separation because, ultimately, the U.S. Constitution, which the Court is entrusted to guard and interpret, is humanistic. It starts with "We the people . . . do ordain and establish" and there isn't a single mention of deities or divine blessings needed for us to prosper. It mentions religion just twice, and both times the word "no" is attached. The first mention is in Article VI that "no religious test shall ever be required." The second time is in the First Amendment of the Bill of Rights: "Congress shall make no law respecting an establishment of religion or prohibiting the free exercise thereof." And so the Constitution is a religiously neutral, secular, and political document.

| "The Constitutional guarantee of
governmental neutrality on religion
has become warped by school officials
fearful of costly lawsuits."

A Plaintiff in the *Schempp* Case Regrets Its Legacy

Kent Demaret

In the following viewpoint Kent Demaret recounts the change of heart of one of the student plaintiffs in the 1963 US Supreme Court case of Abington Township v. Schempp. *William J. Murray III is the son of the atheist activist Madalyn Murray O'Hair. Murray and his mother filed a lawsuit in Maryland against Baltimore's school policy of starting the school day with the reading of Bible passages or the recitation of the Lord's Prayer. This case,* Murray v. Curlett, *was eventually consolidated with the* Schempp *case, and the Court concluded that such religious practices in public school were unconstitutional. Demaret claims Murray believes that the interpretation of the ruling has gone too far and now supports a constitutional amendment allowing school prayer. Murray is chairman of the Religious Freedom Coalition, a nonprofit organization dedicated to the freedom of religious expression. Demaret was the Houston bureau chief for* People *magazine from 1974 to 1992.*

Kent Demaret, "Once the Boy Behind the Ban on School Prayers, Bill Murray Now Prays for a National Change of Heart," *People Weekly*, vol. 21, March 26, 1984, p. 49. Reproduced by permission.

William J. Murray III, now 37 [in 1984], has traveled far from a time more than two decades ago when, as a gawky Baltimore teenager, he was at the center of the landmark Supreme Court test on school prayers. The issues raised in the case never entirely ebbed and now appear to be cresting anew. Congress has begun debate on proposed Constitutional amendments, including one drafted by the Reagan White House, to permit voluntary prayers in public schools. And this is shaping up as a highly emotional issue of the 1984 Presidential election year.

The 1963 US Supreme Court Case

With reservations, Murray favors a school-prayer amendment, a stance at odds with his atheist mother, Madalyn Murray O'Hair, now 64. Mother and son have been estranged for seven years, and subsequently Bill abandoned atheism for evangelism. (O'Hair's younger son, Jon Garth Murray, remains an atheist and is active in his mother's organization, the American Atheist Center.) However, Murray's present position is based less on his own change of heart than on what he insists has been widespread misinterpretation of the 1963 Supreme Court decision [*Abington Township v. Schempp*] in which he was involved.

He was in public school in 1960, when it was fairly customary in the U.S. to begin each day with a prayer. Young Bill, professing atheism, was allowed to stand in the hallway until the prayer was over. If that procedure made Bill Murray uncomfortable, it enraged his mother, who sued to stop the prayers. Ultimately the Supreme Court ruled that young Bill's hallway banishment was a form of coercive pressure and therefore unconstitutional.

Murray contends that this narrow decision meant only that students could not be forced to pray. But over time, he notes with dismay, it has been interpreted by the public as a ban against all school prayers. Meanwhile, according to Murray, the Constitutional guarantee of governmental neutrality on religion has become warped by school officials fearful of costly lawsuits. He cites the example of seven students, all from the same church:

"At the school bus each morning they decided to have a little word of prayer. The school officials found out and told them to stop and desist." He also points to his attempt in January [1984] to rent a school auditorium in Wappingers Falls, N.Y.: "It was a public assembly open to anyone, but the newspaper there said we were going to talk about God in the building, and that it was against the Constitution. Well, it's not, but they denied me anyway."

A School-Prayer Amendment

Such bureaucratic insensibility, he says, has resulted in a general perception of "governmental hostility toward religion, not

Madalyn Murray O'Hair filed suit in 1963 on behalf of her sons William (left) and Jon Garth, protesting their school's practice of starting the day with a religious prayer. © AP Images.

neutrality." To redress that imbalance, he regretfully supports the idea of a school-prayer amendment. "It must be done to satisfy the public backlash if we are to have freedom of religion," he argues. "If the Constitution were properly interpreted, then these amendments would be unnecessary."

Laurence H. Tribe, Tyler Professor of Constitutional Law at Harvard, who opposes any amendment, agrees about the Constitution. "The premise that prayer is not allowed in schools," he says, "is a lie. Official, organized prayer is not allowed, true, but kids can pray if they want." Indeed, some legal scholars think that the conflict within the First Amendment might be resolved ultimately by allowing a moment of silence.

Murray sees his challenge as the conversion of atheists and agnostics rather than Constitutional issues. Twice divorced and a recovering alcoholic since 1978, he lives alone in Garland, Texas, near Dallas. For three years he has been an active Baptist (though not a minister), and he now says what his family did was "a criminal act," which has driven him to seek atonement. His vehicle is the Murray Faith Ministries, a nonprofit, contribution-supported religious organization from which he draws a $1,400 monthly salary and for which he traveled 43,000 miles last year as its sole evangelist. He draws on his own experience: "I tell them I have walked in their shoes. And I can tell them they are on a dead-end road leading to sadness, emptiness and an unfulfilled life." Next month Madalyn Murray O'Hair is scheduled to head an atheist convention in Lexington, [Kentucky]. Bill Murray plans to be there, too, to conduct counter-rallies.

"I have become peaceful in the last few years," he says. Perhaps, but the explosive religious issues that he once helped to spark remain at flash point all around him.

> *"Compulsory formal education after the
> eighth grade would gravely endanger,
> if not destroy, the free exercise of
> respondents' religious beliefs."*

Compulsory School Attendance Laws Violate the Rights of the Amish

The Supreme Court's Decision

Warren E. Burger

In the following viewpoint Chief Justice Warren E. Burger, writing for the majority of the Court, held that a compulsory school attendance law in Wisconsin was unconstitutional as applied to the Amish people. The Court contends that because education after the eighth grade goes against the fundamental religious beliefs of the Amish people, the state may not compel attendance of Amish children of that age. The Court emphasizes that the state has an interest in the education of children, in general, which often supports the state's right to implement compulsory school attendance laws. It is only in the case of such laws violating the free exercise of religion that the state's interest may not be absolute. The Court concludes that there is no compelling interest to override the Amish right to free exercise in this case, since the Amish are a successful

Warren E. Burger, Majority opinion, *Wisconsin v. Yoder*, US Supreme Court, May 15, 1972. Copyright © 1972 The Supreme Court of the United States.

people despite engaging in formal schooling only through eighth
grade. Burger was chief justice of the US Supreme Court from 1969
until his retirement in 1986.

Respondents Jonas Yoder and Wallace Miller are members of the Old Order Amish religion, and respondent Adin Yutzy is a member of the Conservative Amish Mennonite Church. They and their families are residents of Green County, Wisconsin. Wisconsin's compulsory school attendance law required them to cause their children to attend public or private school until reaching age 16, but the respondents declined to send their children, ages 14 and 15, to public school after they completed the eighth grade. The children were not enrolled in any private school, or within any recognized exception to the compulsory attendance law, and they are conceded to be subject to the Wisconsin statute.

Objection to a Compulsory Attendance Law

On complaint of the school district administrator for the public schools, respondents were charged, tried, and convicted of violating the compulsory attendance law in Green County Court, and were fined the sum of $5 each. Respondents defended on the ground that the application of the compulsory attendance law violated their rights under the First and Fourteenth Amendments. The trial testimony showed that respondents believed, in accordance with the tenets of Old Order Amish communities generally, that their children's attendance at high school, public or private, was contrary to the Amish religion and way of life. They believed that, by sending their children to high school, they would not only expose themselves to the danger of the censure of the church community, but, as found by the county court, also endanger their own salvation and that of their children. The State stipulated that respondents' religious beliefs were sincere.

In support of their position, respondents presented as expert witnesses scholars on religion and education whose testimony is uncontradicted. They expressed their opinions on the relationship of the Amish belief concerning school attendance to the more general tenets of their religion, and described the impact that compulsory high school attendance could have on the continued survival of Amish communities as they exist in the United States today. The history of the Amish sect was given in some detail, beginning with the Swiss Anabaptists of the 16th century, who rejected institutionalized churches and sought to return to the early, simple, Christian life deemphasizing material success, rejecting the competitive spirit, and seeking to insulate themselves from the modern world. As a result of their common heritage, Old Order Amish communities today are characterized by a fundamental belief that salvation requires life in a church community separate and apart from the world and worldly influence. This concept of life aloof from the world and its values is central to their faith. . . .

Amish objection to formal education beyond the eighth grade is firmly grounded in these central religious concepts. They object to the high school, and higher education generally, because the values they teach are in marked variance with Amish values and the Amish way of life; they view secondary school education as an impermissible exposure of their children to a "worldly" influence in conflict with their beliefs. The high school tends to emphasize intellectual and scientific accomplishments, self-distinction, competitiveness, worldly success, and social life with other students. Amish society emphasizes informal "learning through doing"; a life of "goodness," rather than a life of intellect; wisdom, rather than technical knowledge; community welfare, rather than competition; and separation from, rather than integration with, contemporary worldly society.

The Amish Objection to High School

Formal high school education beyond the eighth grade is contrary to Amish beliefs not only because it places Amish children

AMISH POPULATION IN NORTH AMERICA, 2010

State	Number of Church Districts	Amish Population
Arkansas	3	225
Colorado	6	810
Delaware	9	1,350
Florida	1	75
Illinois	49	6,860
Indiana	310	43,710
Iowa	51	7,190
Kansas	11	1,485
Kentucky	62	7,750
Maine	3	225
Maryland	10	1,350
Michigan	86	11,350
Minnesota	25	3,150
Mississippi	1	75
Missouri	81	9,475
Montana	5	675
Nebraska	2	150
New York	89	12,015
North Carolina	1	75
Ohio	434	58,590
Oklahoma	5	675
Ontario	35	4,725
Pennsylvania	401	59,350
South Dakota	1	75
Tennessee	17	2,125
Texas	1	75
Virginia	4	300
West Virginia	3	225
Wisconsin	120	15,360

Taken from: Timothy Aeppel, "The Amish Population Boom," *Wall Street Journal*, July 29, 2010.

in an environment hostile to Amish beliefs, with increasing emphasis on competition in class work and sports, and with pressure to conform to the styles, manners, and ways of the peer group, but also because it takes them away from their community, physically and emotionally, during the crucial and formative adolescent period of life. During this period, the children must acquire Amish attitudes favoring manual work and self-reliance and the specific skills needed to perform the adult role of an Amish farmer or housewife. They must learn to enjoy physical labor. Once a child has learned basic reading, writing, and elementary mathematics, these traits, skills, and attitudes admittedly fall within the category of those best learned through example and "doing," rather than in a classroom. And, at this time in life, the Amish child must also grow in his faith and his relationship to the Amish community if he is to be prepared to accept the heavy obligations imposed by adult baptism. In short, high school attendance with teachers who are not of the Amish faith—and may even be hostile to it—interposes a serious barrier to the integration of the Amish child into the Amish religious community. Dr. John Hostetler, one of the experts on Amish society, testified that the modern high school is not equipped, in curriculum or social environment, to impart the values promoted by Amish society.

The Amish do not object to elementary education through the first eight grades as a general proposition, because they agree that their children must have basic skills in the "three R's" in order to read the Bible, to be good farmers and citizens, and to be able to deal with non-Amish people when necessary in the course of daily affairs. They view such a basic education as acceptable because it does not significantly expose their children to worldly values or interfere with their development in the Amish

---

Members of the Amish community argued against compulsory school attendance, stating that modern high schools do not prepare Amish teenagers for life within the traditional Amish community and may damage their chance of salvation. © William Albert Allard/National Geographic/Getty Images.

community during the crucial adolescent period. While Amish accept compulsory elementary education generally, wherever possible, they have established their own elementary schools, in many respects like the small local schools of the past. In the Amish belief, higher learning tends to develop values they reject as influences that alienate man from God.

On the basis of such considerations, Dr. Hostetler testified that compulsory high school attendance could not only result in great psychological harm to Amish children, because of the conflicts it would produce, but would also, in his opinion, ultimately result in the destruction of the Old Order Amish church community as it exists in the United States today. The testimony of Dr. Donald A. Erickson, an expert witness on education, also showed that the Amish succeed in preparing their high school age children to be productive members of the Amish community. He described their system of learning through doing the skills directly relevant to their adult roles in the Amish community as "ideal," and perhaps superior to ordinary high school education. The evidence also showed that the Amish have an excellent record as law-abiding and generally self-sufficient members of society. . . .

The State Interest in Education

There is no doubt as to the power of a State, having a high responsibility for education of its citizens, to impose reasonable regulations for the control and duration of basic education. Providing public schools ranks at the very apex of the function of a State. Yet even this paramount responsibility was, in *Pierce* [*v. Society of Sisters* (1925)], made to yield to the right of parents to provide an equivalent education in a privately operated system. There, the Court held that Oregon's statute compelling attendance in a public school from age eight to age 16 unreasonably interfered with the interest of parents in directing the rearing of their offspring, including their education in church-operated schools. As that case suggests, the values of parental direction of the religious upbringing and education of their children in their early and formative years have a high place in our society. Thus, a State's interest in universal education, however highly we rank it, is not totally free from a balancing process when it impinges on fundamental rights and interests, such as those specifically protected by the Free Exercise Clause of the First Amendment, and the traditional interest of parents with respect to the religious upbringing of their children so long as they, in the words of *Pierce*, "prepare [them] for additional obligations."

It follows that, in order for Wisconsin to compel school attendance beyond the eighth grade against a claim that such attendance interferes with the practice of a legitimate religious belief, it must appear either that the State does not deny the free exercise of religious belief by its requirement or that there is a State interest of sufficient magnitude to override the interest claiming protection under the Free Exercise Clause. Long before there was general acknowledgment of the need for universal formal education, the Religion Clauses had specifically and firmly fixed the right to free exercise of religious beliefs, and buttressing this fundamental right was an equally firm, even if less explicit, prohibition against the establishment of any religion by government. The values underlying these two provisions relating to religion have been zealously protected, sometimes even at the expense of other interests of admittedly high social importance. The invalidation of financial aid to parochial schools by government grants for a salary subsidy for teachers is but one example of the extent to which courts have gone in this regard, notwithstanding that such aid programs were legislatively determined to be in the public interest and the service of sound educational policy by States and by Congress.

The essence of all that has been said and written on the subject is that only those interests of the highest order and those not otherwise served can overbalance legitimate claims to the free exercise of religion. We can accept it as settled, therefore, that, however strong the State's interest in universal compulsory education, it is by no means absolute to the exclusion or subordination of all other interests.

The Right to Free Exercise

We come then to the quality of the claims of the respondents concerning the alleged encroachment of Wisconsin's compulsory school attendance statute on their rights and the rights of their children to the free exercise of the religious beliefs they and their forebears have adhered to for almost three centuries. In evaluating those claims, we must be careful to determine whether the Amish religious faith and their mode of life are, as they claim, inseparable and interdependent. A way of life, however virtuous and admirable, may not be interposed as a barrier to reasonable State regulation of education if it is based on purely secular considerations; to have the protection of the Religion Clauses, the claims must be rooted in religious belief. Although a determination of what is a "religious" belief or practice entitled to constitutional protection may present a most delicate question, the very concept of ordered liberty precludes allowing every person to make his own standards on matters of conduct in which society as a whole has important interests. Thus, if the Amish asserted their claims because of their subjective evaluation and rejection of the contemporary secular values accepted by the majority, much as [Henry David]Thoreau rejected the social values of his time and isolated himself at Walden Pond, their claims would not rest on a religious basis. Thoreau's choice was philosophical and personal, rather than religious, and such belief does not rise to the demands of the Religion Clauses.

Giving no weight to such secular considerations, however, we see that the record in this case abundantly supports the claim that the traditional way of life of the Amish is not merely a matter of personal preference, but one of deep religious conviction, shared by an organized group, and intimately related to daily living. . . .

As the society around the Amish has become more populous, urban, industrialized, and complex, particularly in this century, government regulation of human affairs has correspondingly become more detailed and pervasive. The Amish mode of life has thus come into conflict increasingly with requirements of contemporary society exerting a hydraulic insistence on conformity to majoritarian standards. So long as compulsory education laws were confined to eight grades of elementary basic education imparted in a nearby rural schoolhouse, with a large proportion of students of the Amish faith, the Old Order Amish had little basis to fear that school attendance would expose their children to the worldly influence they reject. But modern compulsory secondary education in rural areas is now largely carried on in a consolidated school, often remote from the student's home and alien to his daily home life. As the record so strongly shows, the values and programs of the modern secondary school are in sharp conflict with the fundamental mode of life mandated by the Amish religion; modern laws requiring compulsory secondary education have accordingly engendered great concern and conflict. The conclusion is inescapable that secondary schooling, by exposing Amish children to worldly influences in terms of attitudes, goals, and values contrary to beliefs, and by substantially interfering with the religious development of the Amish child and his integration into the way of life of the Amish faith community at the crucial adolescent stage of development, contravenes the basic religious tenets and practice of the Amish faith, both as to the parent and the child.

The impact of the compulsory attendance law on respondents' practice of the Amish religion is not only severe, but inescapable, for the Wisconsin law affirmatively compels them, under threat of criminal sanction, to perform acts undeniably at odds with fundamental tenets of their religious beliefs. Nor is the impact of the compulsory attendance law confined to grave interference with important Amish religious tenets from a subjective point of view. It carries with it precisely the kind of objective danger to the free exercise of religion that the First Amendment was designed to prevent. As the record shows, compulsory school attendance to age 16 for Amish children carries with it a very real threat of undermining the Amish community and religious practice as they exist today; they must either abandon belief and be assimilated into society at large or be forced to migrate to some other and more tolerant region.

In sum, the unchallenged testimony of acknowledged experts in education and religious history, almost 300 years of consistent practice, and strong evidence of a sustained faith pervading and regulating respondents' entire mode of life support the claim that enforcement of the State's requirement of compulsory formal education after the eighth grade would gravely endanger, if not destroy, the free exercise of respondents' religious beliefs. . . .

The State's Arguments

The State advances two primary arguments in support of its system of compulsory education. It notes, as Thomas Jefferson pointed out early in our history, that some degree of education is necessary to prepare citizens to participate effectively and intelligently in our open political system if we are to preserve freedom and independence. Further, education prepares individuals to be self-reliant and self-sufficient participants in society. We accept these propositions.

However, the evidence adduced by the Amish in this case is persuasively to the effect that an additional one or two years of formal high school for Amish children in place of their long-established program of informal vocational education would do little to serve those interests. Respondents' experts testified at trial, without challenge, that the value of all education must be assessed in terms of its capacity to prepare the child for life. It is one thing to say that compulsory education for a year or two beyond the eighth grade may be necessary when its goal is the preparation of the child for life in modern society as the majority live, but it is quite another if the goal of education be viewed as the preparation of the child for life in the separated agrarian community that is the keystone of the Amish faith.

The State attacks respondents' position as one fostering "ignorance" from which the child must be protected by the State. No one can question the State's duty to protect children from ignorance, but this argument does not square with the facts disclosed in the record. Whatever their idiosyncrasies as seen by the majority, this record strongly shows that the Amish community has been a highly successful social unit within our society, even if apart from the conventional "mainstream." Its members are productive and very law-abiding members of society; they reject public welfare in any of its usual modern forms. The Congress itself recognized their self-sufficiency by authorizing exemption of such groups as the Amish from the obligation to pay social security taxes. . . .

For the reasons stated we hold, with the Supreme Court of Wisconsin, that the First and Fourteenth Amendments prevent the State from compelling respondents to cause their children to attend formal high school to age 16. Our disposition of this case, however, in no way alters our recognition of the obvious fact that courts are not school boards or legislatures, and are ill-equipped to determine the "necessity" of discrete aspects of a State's program of compulsory education. This should suggest that courts must move with great circumspection in performing the sensitive and delicate task of weighing a State's legitimate social concern when faced with religious claims for exemption from generally applicable educational requirements. It cannot be overemphasized that we are not dealing with a way of life and mode of education by a group claiming to have recently discovered some "progressive" or more enlightened process for rearing children for modern life.

> "Kentucky's statute requiring the posting
> of the Ten Commandments in public
> school rooms has no secular legislative
> purpose."

It Is Unconstitutional to Display the Ten Commandments in Public Schools

The Supreme Court's Decision

Per Curiam *opinion (US Supreme Court)*

In the following viewpoint the US Supreme Court determined that public schools may not post copies of the Ten Commandments in classrooms. The Court argues that the Establishment Clause of the First Amendment requires that laws have a secular purpose that does not advance or hinder religion. The Court claims that posting the Ten Commandments clearly has a religious purpose. Furthermore, the Court claims that even if the copies of the Ten Commandments are financed privately, this condition does not alleviate the worry about the state unconstitutionally advancing religion in public schools. The US Supreme Court is the highest judicial body in the United States.

Per Curium opinion, *Stone v. Graham*, US Supreme Court, November 17, 1980. Copyright © 1980 The Supreme Court of the United States.

Kentucky statute requires the posting of a copy of the Ten Commandments, purchased with private contributions, on the wall of each public classroom in the State. Petitioners, claiming that this statute violates the Establishment and Free Exercise Clauses of the First Amendment, sought an injunction against its enforcement. The State trial court upheld the statute, finding that its "avowed purpose" was "secular and not religious," and that the statute would "neither advance nor inhibit any religion or religious group" nor involve the State excessively in religious matters. The Supreme Court of the Commonwealth of Kentucky affirmed by an equally divided court. We reverse.

A Secular Legislative Purpose

This Court has announced a three-part test for determining whether a challenged State statute is permissible under the Establishment Clause of the United States Constitution:

> First, the statute must have a secular legislative purpose; second, its principal or primary effect must be one that neither advances nor inhibits religion . . . ; finally the statute must not foster "an excessive government entanglement with religion" [*Lemon v. Kurtzman* (1971)].

If a statute violates any of these three principles, it must be struck down under the Establishment Clause. We conclude that Kentucky's statute requiring the posting of the Ten Commandments in public school rooms has no secular legislative purpose, and is therefore unconstitutional.

The Commonwealth insists that the statute in question serves a secular legislative purpose, observing that the legislature required the following notation in small print at the bottom of each display of the Ten Commandments:

> The secular application of the Ten Commandments is clearly seen in its adoption as the fundamental legal code of Western Civilization and the Common Law of the United States.

The trial court found the "avowed" purpose of the statute to be secular, even as it labeled the statutory declaration "self-serving." Under this Court's rulings, however, such an "avowed" secular purpose is not sufficient to avoid conflict with the First Amendment. In *Abington School District v. Schempp* (1963), this Court held unconstitutional the daily reading of Bible verses and the Lord's Prayer in the public schools, despite the school district's assertion of such secular purposes as

> the promotion of moral values, the contradiction to the materialistic trends of our times, the perpetuation of our institutions and the teaching of literature.

An Unconstitutional Religious Purpose

The preeminent purpose for posting the Ten Commandments on schoolroom walls is plainly religious in nature. The Ten Commandments are undeniably a sacred text in the Jewish and

Protesters at a rally in Washington, D.C., hold signs supporting the display of the Ten Commandments on government property. The Supreme Court ruled that such signs violate the Establishment Clause when displayed at public schools. © Alex Wong/Getty Images.

The Unconstitutional Kentucky Statute

(1) It shall be the duty of the superintendent of public instruction, provided sufficient funds are available as provided in subsection (3) of this Section, to ensure that a durable, permanent copy of the Ten Commandments shall be displayed on a wall in each public elementary and secondary school classroom in the Commonwealth. The copy shall be sixteen (16) inches wide by twenty (20) inches high.

(2) In small print below the last commandment shall appear a notation concerning the purpose of the display, as follows: "The secular application of the Ten Commandments is clearly seen in its adoption as the fundamental legal code of Western Civilization and the Common Law of the United States."

(3) The copies required by this Act shall be purchased with funds made available through voluntary contributions made to the state treasurer for the purposes of this Act.

1978 Ky. Acts, ch. 436, § 1 (effective June 17, 1978), Ky.Rev.Stat. § 158.78 (1980)

Christian faiths, and no legislative recitation of a supposed secular purpose can blind us to that fact. The Commandments do not confine themselves to arguably secular matters, such as honoring one's parents, killing or murder, adultery, stealing, false witness, and covetousness. Rather, the first part of the Commandments concerns the religious duties of believers: worshipping the Lord God alone, avoiding idolatry, not using the Lord's name in vain, and observing the Sabbath Day.

This is not a case in which the Ten Commandments are integrated into the school curriculum, where the Bible may constitutionally be used in an appropriate study of history, civilization, ethics, comparative religion, or the like. Posting of religious texts on the wall serves no such educational function. If the posted copies of the Ten Commandments are to have any effect at all, it will be to induce the schoolchildren to read, meditate upon, perhaps to venerate and obey, the Commandments. However desirable this might be as a matter of private devotion, it is not a permissible state objective under the Establishment Clause.

It does not matter that the posted copies of the Ten Commandments are financed by voluntary private contributions, for the mere posting of the copies under the auspices of the legislature provides the "official support of the State . . . Government" that the Establishment Clause prohibits. Nor is it significant that the Bible verses involved in this case are merely posted on the wall, rather than read aloud as in *Schempp* and *Engel* [*v. Vitale* (1962)], for "it is no defense to urge that the religious practices here may be relatively minor encroachments on the First Amendment." We conclude that Ky.Rev.Stat. § 158.178 (1980) violates the first part of the *Lemon v. Kurtzman* test, and thus the Establishment Clause of the Constitution.

| *"The government must pursue a course of complete neutrality toward religion."*

It Is Unconstitutional for Public Schools to Require a Moment of Silence for Voluntary Prayer

The Supreme Court's Decision

John Paul Stevens

In the following viewpoint Justice John Paul Stevens, writing for the majority of the Court, argues that a state statute authorizing a moment of silence for meditation or voluntary prayer is unconstitutional precisely because the intent of the statute was to promote school prayer. The Court distinguished such a statute from a previous one in which a moment of silence was authorized for meditation, determining that because the legislature enacted a new statute changed only by putting in the option of prayer, the government did not have a secular purpose for enacting the law, as required by the Establishment Clause of the First Amendment. Stevens served as associate justice of the US Supreme Court from 1975 until his retirement in 2010.

John Paul Stevens, Majority opinion, *Wallace v. Jaffree*, US Supreme Court, June 4, 1985. Copyright © 1985 The Supreme Court of the United States.

At an early stage of this litigation, the constitutionality of three Alabama statutes was questioned: (1) § 16-1-20, enacted in 1978, which authorized a 1-minute period of silence in all public schools "for meditation"; (2) § 16-1-20.1, enacted in 1981, which authorized a period of silence "for meditation or voluntary prayer"; and (3) § 16-1-20.2, enacted in 1982, which authorized teachers to lead "willing students" in a prescribed prayer to "Almighty God . . . the Creator and Supreme Judge of the world."

At the preliminary injunction stage of this case, the District Court distinguished § 16-1-20 from the other two statutes. It then held that there was "nothing wrong" with § 16-1-20, but that §§ 16-1-20.1 and 16-1-20.2 were both invalid because the sole purpose of both was "an effort on the part of the State of Alabama to encourage a religious activity." After the trial on the merits, the District Court did not change its interpretation of these two statutes, but held that they were constitutional because, in its opinion, Alabama has the power to establish a state religion if it chooses to do so.

A Consideration of a Voluntary Prayer Statute

The Court of Appeals agreed with the District Court's initial interpretation of the purpose of both § 16-1-20.1 and § 16-1-20.2, and held them both unconstitutional. We have already affirmed the Court of Appeals' holding with respect to § 16-1-20.2. Moreover, appellees have not questioned the holding that § 16-1-20 is valid. Thus, the narrow question for decision is whether § 16-1-20.1, which authorizes a period of silence for "meditation or voluntary prayer," is a law respecting the establishment of religion within the meaning of the First Amendment.

Appellee Ishmael Jaffree is a resident of Mobile County, Alabama. On May 28, 1982, he filed a complaint on behalf of three of his minor children; two of them were second-grade students and the third was then in kindergarten. The complaint named members of the Mobile County School Board, various school officials, and the minor plaintiffs' three teachers as defendants. The complaint alleged that the appellees brought the action

> seeking principally a declaratory judgment and an injunction restraining the Defendants and each of them from maintaining or allowing the maintenance of regular religious prayer services or other forms of religious observances in the Mobile County Public Schools in violation of the First Amendment as made applicable to states by the Fourteenth Amendment to the United States Constitution.

The complaint further alleged that two of the children had been subjected to various acts of religious indoctrination "from the beginning of the school year in September, 1981"; that the defendant teachers had "on a daily basis" led their classes in saying certain prayers in unison; that the minor children were exposed to ostracism from their peer group class members if they did not participate; and that Ishmael Jaffree had repeatedly but unsuccessfully requested that the devotional services be stopped. The original complaint made no reference to any Alabama statute. . . .

Freedom from Government Religion

Just as the right to speak and the right to refrain from speaking are complementary components of a broader concept of individual freedom of mind, so also the individual's freedom to choose his own creed is the counterpart of his right to refrain from accepting the creed established by the majority. At one time, it was thought that this right merely proscribed the preference of one Christian sect over another, but would not require equal respect for the conscience of the infidel, the atheist, or the adherent of a non-Christian faith such as Islam or Judaism. But when the underlying principle has been examined in the crucible of litigation, the Court has unambiguously concluded that the individual freedom of conscience protected by the First Amendment embraces the right to select any religious faith or none at all. This conclusion derives support not only from the interest in respecting the individual's freedom of conscience, but also from the conviction that religious beliefs worthy of respect are the product of free and voluntary choice by the faithful, and from recognition of the fact that the political interest in forestalling intolerance extends beyond intolerance among Christian sects—or even intolerance among "religions"—to encompass intolerance of the disbeliever and the uncertain. As Justice Jackson eloquently stated in *West Virginia Board of Education v. Barnette* (1943):

> If there is any fixed star in our constitutional constellation [any controlling principle among our founding principles], it is that no official, high or petty, can prescribe what shall be orthodox in politics, nationalism, religion, or other matters of opinion or force citizens to confess by word or act their faith therein.

The State of Alabama, no less than the Congress of the United States, must respect that basic truth.

When the Court has been called upon to construe the breadth of the Establishment Clause, it has examined the criteria developed over a period of many years. Thus, in *Lemon v. Kurtzman* (1971), we wrote:

> Every analysis in this area must begin with consideration of the cumulative criteria developed by the Court over many years. Three such tests may be gleaned from our cases. First, the statute must have a secular legislative purpose; second, its principal or primary effect must be one that neither advances nor inhibits religion; finally, the statute must not foster "an excessive government entanglement with religion."

It is the first of these three criteria that is most plainly implicated by this case. As the District Court correctly recognized, no consideration of the second or third criteria is necessary if a statute does not have a clearly secular purpose. For even though a statute that is motivated in part by a religious purpose may

SUPPORT FOR AN AMENDMENT TO ALLOW VOLUNTARY PRAYER IN PUBLIC SCHOOLS

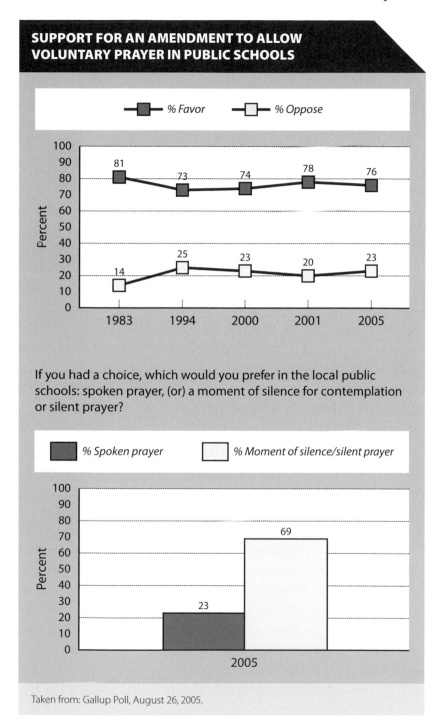

If you had a choice, which would you prefer in the local public schools: spoken prayer, (or) a moment of silence for contemplation or silent prayer?

Taken from: Gallup Poll, August 26, 2005.

satisfy the first criterion, the First Amendment requires that a statute must be invalidated if it is entirely motivated by a purpose to advance religion.

The Need for a Secular Purpose

In applying the purpose test, it is appropriate to ask "whether government's actual purpose is to endorse or disapprove of religion." In this case, the answer to that question is dispositive. For the record not only provides us with an unambiguous affirmative answer, but it also reveals that the enactment of § 16-1-20.1 was not motivated by any clearly secular purpose; indeed, the statute had *no* secular purpose.

The sponsor of the bill that became § 16-1-20.1, Senator Donald Holmes, inserted into the legislative record—apparently without dissent—a statement indicating that the legislation was an "effort to return voluntary prayer" to the public schools. Later Senator Holmes confirmed this purpose before the District Court. In response to the question whether he had any purpose for the legislation other than returning voluntary prayer to public schools, he stated: "No, I did not have no other purpose in mind." The State did not present evidence of *any* secular purpose.

The unrebutted evidence of legislative intent contained in the legislative record and in the testimony of the sponsor of § 16-1-20.1 is confirmed by a consideration of the relationship between this statute and the two other measures that were considered in this case. The District Court found that the 1981 statute and its 1982 sequel had a common, nonsecular purpose. The wholly religious character of the later enactment is plainly evident from its text. When the differences between § 16-1-20.1 and its 1978 predecessor, § 16-1-20, are examined, it is equally clear that the 1981 statute has the same wholly religious character.

There are only three textual differences between § 16-1-20.1 and § 16-1-20: (1) the earlier statute applies only to grades one through six, whereas § 16-1-20.1 applies to all grades; (2) the earlier statute uses the word "shall" whereas § 16-1-20.1 uses the

A sixth-grader participates in a moment of silence at Northeastern Academy in Oklahoma City. Policies mandating such observances at public schools have been ruled unconstitutional when their purpose is to create a favored status for prayer. © AP Images/Andrew Laker.

word "may"; (3) the earlier statute refers only to "meditation" whereas § 16-1-20.1 refers to "meditation or voluntary prayer." The first difference is of no relevance in this litigation, because the minor appellees were in kindergarten or second grade during the 1981–1982 academic year. The second difference would also have no impact on this litigation, because the mandatory language of § 16-1-20 continued to apply to grades one through six. Thus, the only significant textual difference is the addition of the words "or voluntary prayer."

The Legislative Intent

The legislative intent to return prayer to the public schools is, of course, quite different from merely protecting every student's right to engage in voluntary prayer during an appropriate moment of silence during the school day. The 1978 statute already protected that right, containing nothing that prevented any student from engaging in voluntary prayer during a silent minute of meditation. Appellants have not identified any secular purpose that was not fully served by § 16-1-20 before the enactment of § 16-1-20.1. Thus, only two conclusions are consistent with the text of § 16-1-20.1: (1) the statute was enacted to convey a message of state endorsement and promotion of prayer; or (2) the statute was enacted for no purpose. No one suggests that the statute was nothing but a meaningless or irrational act.

We must, therefore, conclude that the Alabama Legislature intended to change existing law, and that it was motivated by the same purpose that the Governor's answer to the second amended complaint expressly admitted; that the statement inserted in the legislative history revealed; and that Senator Holmes' testimony frankly described. The legislature enacted § 16-1-20.1, despite the existence of § 16-1-20, for the sole purpose of expressing the State's endorsement of prayer activities for one minute at the beginning of each school day. The addition of "or voluntary prayer" indicates that the State intended to characterize prayer as a favored practice. Such an endorsement is not consistent with the established principle that the government must pursue a course of complete neutrality toward religion.

The importance of that principle does not permit us to treat this as an inconsequential case involving nothing more than a few words of symbolic speech on behalf of the political majority. For whenever the State itself speaks on a religious subject, one of the questions that we must ask is "whether the government intends to convey a message of endorsement or disapproval of religion" [*Lynch v. Donnelly* (1984) (Justice O'Connor concurring)]. The well-supported concurrent findings of the District Court and the Court of Appeals—that § 16-1-20.1 was intended to convey a message of state approval of prayer activities in the public schools—make it unnecessary, and indeed inappropriate, to evaluate the practical significance of the addition of the words "or voluntary prayer" to the statute. Keeping in mind, as we must,

> both the fundamental place held by the Establishment Clause in our constitutional scheme and the myriad, subtle ways in which Establishment Clause values can be eroded,

we conclude that § 16-1-20.1 violates the First Amendment.

> "No holding by this Court suggests that a school can persuade or compel a student to participate in a religious exercise."

Religious Authorities May Not Lead Prayers at Public School Graduations

The Supreme Court's Decision

Anthony Kennedy

In the following viewpoint Justice Anthony Kennedy, writing for the majority of the Court, contends that a decision by school authorities to authorize a religious leader—a rabbi—to give a nonsectarian prayer at a public school graduation ceremony violates the First Amendment of the US Constitution. The Court emphasizes that government officials—in this case, public school officials—may not in any way sponsor or direct a religious exercise in public school. The Court denies that nonsectarian prayer—even though it is not associated with any particular religion—is consistent with the First Amendment, as government officials may not prescribe any kind of prayer. The Court concludes that its opinion is not meant to completely expunge personal prayer from public school activities, but emphasizes that prayer sponsored by school

Anthony Kennedy, Majority opinion, *Lee v. Weisman*, US Supreme Court, June 24, 1992.

*officials and implemented in a situation where students are com-
pelled to participate violates the Establishment Clause of the First
Amendment. Kennedy is an associate justice of the US Supreme
Court, appointed by Ronald Reagan in 1988.*

Deborah Weisman graduated from Nathan Bishop Middle
School, a public school in Providence, [Rhode Island], at
a formal ceremony in June 1989. She was about 14 years old.
For many years it has been the policy of the Providence School
Committee and the Superintendent of Schools to permit principals to invite members of the clergy to give invocations and
benedictions at middle school and high school graduations.
Many, but not all, of the principals elected to include prayers as
part of the graduation ceremonies. Acting for himself and his
daughter, Deborah's father, Daniel Weisman, objected to any
prayers at Deborah's middle school graduation, but to no avail.
The school principal, petitioner Robert E. Lee, invited a rabbi to
deliver prayers at the graduation exercises for Deborah's class.
Rabbi Leslie Gutterman, of the Temple Beth El in Providence,
accepted.

A Prayer at a Public School Graduation

It has been the custom of Providence school officials to provide
invited clergy with a pamphlet entitled "Guidelines for Civic
Occasions," prepared by the National Conference of Christians
and Jews. The [guidelines] recommend that public prayers at
nonsectarian civic ceremonies be composed with "inclusiveness
and sensitivity," though they acknowledge that "[p]rayer of any
kind may be inappropriate on some civic occasions." The principal gave Rabbi Gutterman the pamphlet before the graduation and advised him the invocation and benediction should be
nonsectarian.

Rabbi Gutterman's prayers were as follows:

"INVOCATION

"God of the Free, Hope of the Brave:

"For the legacy of America where diversity is celebrated and the rights of minorities are protected, we thank You. May these young men and women grow up to enrich it.

"For the liberty of America, we thank You. May these new graduates grow up to guard it.

"For the political process of America in which all its citizens may participate, for its court system where all may seek justice we thank You. May those we honor this morning always turn to it in trust.

"For the destiny of America we thank You. May the graduates of Nathan Bishop Middle School so live that they might help to share it.

"May our aspirations for our country and for these young people, who are our hope for the future, be richly fulfilled.

"AMEN"

"BENEDICTION

"O God, we are grateful to You for having endowed us with the capacity for learning which we have celebrated on this joyous commencement.

"Happy families give thanks for seeing their children achieve an important milestone. Send Your blessings upon the teachers and administrators who helped prepare them.

"The graduates now need strength and guidance for the future, help them to understand that we are not complete with academic knowledge alone. We must each strive to fulfill what You require of us all: To do justly, to love mercy, to walk humbly.

"We give thanks to You, Lord, for keeping us alive, sustaining us and allowing us to reach this special, happy occasion.

"AMEN"

The record in this case is sparse in many respects, and we are unfamiliar with any fixed custom or practice at middle school graduations, referred to by the school district as "promotional ex-

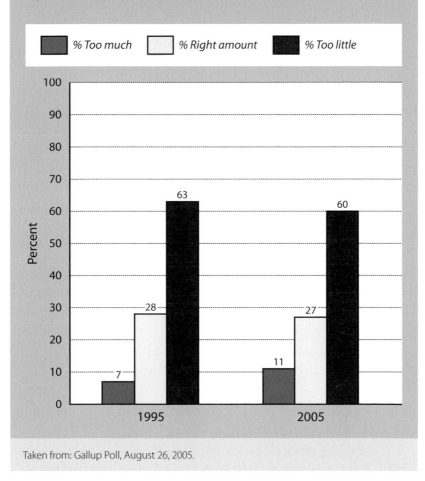

AMERICANS' VIEWS ON RELIGION IN SCHOOL, 1995–2005

Thinking about the presence that religion currently has in public schools in this country, do you think religion has too much of a presence in public schools, about the right amount, (or) too little of a presence in public schools?

■ % Too much   □ % Right amount   ■ % Too little

Percent

Taken from: Gallup Poll, August 26, 2005.

ercises." We are not so constrained with reference to high schools, however. High school graduations are such an integral part of American cultural life that we can with confidence describe their customary features, confirmed by aspects of the record and by the parties' representations at oral argument. In the Providence school system, most high school graduation ceremonies are conducted away from the school, while most middle school ceremonies are held on school premises. Classical High School, which Deborah now attends, has conducted its graduation ceremonies on school premises. The parties stipulate that attendance at graduation ceremonies is voluntary. The graduating students enter as a group in a processional, subject to the direction of teachers and school officials, and sit together, apart from their families. We assume the clergy's participation in any high school graduation exercise would be about what it was at Deborah's middle school ceremony. There the students stood for the Pledge of Allegiance and remained standing during the Rabbi's prayers. Even on the assumption that there was a respectful moment of silence both before and after the prayers, the Rabbi's two presentations must not have extended much beyond a minute each, if that. We do not know whether he remained on stage during the whole ceremony, or whether the students received individual diplomas on stage, or if he helped to congratulate them.

The school board argued that these short prayers and others like them at graduation exercises are of profound meaning to many students and parents throughout this country who consider that due respect and acknowledgement for divine guidance and for the deepest spiritual aspirations of our people ought to be expressed at an event as important in life as a graduation. We assume this to be so in addressing the difficult case now before us, for the significance of the prayers lies also at the heart of Daniel and Deborah Weisman's case.

Deborah's graduation was held on the premises of Nathan Bishop Middle School on June 29, 1989. Four days before the ceremony, Daniel Weisman, in his individual capacity as a Providence taxpayer and as next friend [legal representative] of Deborah, sought a temporary restraining order in the United States District Court for the District of Rhode Island to prohibit school officials from including an invocation or benediction in the graduation ceremony. The court denied the motion for lack of adequate time to consider it. Deborah and her family attended the graduation, where the prayers were recited. In July 1989, Daniel Weisman filed an amended complaint seeking a permanent injunction barring petitioners, various officials of the Providence public schools, from inviting the clergy to deliver invocations and benedictions at future graduations. . . .

Government Involvement with Religious Activity

These dominant facts mark and control the confines of our decision: State officials direct the performance of a formal religious exercise at promotional and graduation ceremonies for secondary schools. Even for those students who object to the religious exercise, their attendance and participation in the state sponsored religious activity are in a fair and real sense obligatory, though the school district does not require attendance as a condition for receipt of the diploma.

This case does not require us to revisit the difficult questions dividing us in recent cases, questions of the definition and full scope of the principles governing the extent of permitted accommodation by the State for the religious beliefs and practices of many of its citizens. For without reference to those principles in other contexts, the controlling precedents as they relate to prayer and religious exercise in primary and secondary public schools compel the holding here that the policy of the city of Providence is an unconstitutional one. We can decide the case without reconsidering the general constitutional framework by which public schools' efforts to accommodate religion are measured. . . . The government involvement with religious activity in this case is pervasive, to the point of creating a state sponsored and state-directed religious exercise in a public school. Conducting this formal religious observance conflicts with settled rules pertaining to prayer exercises for students, and that suffices to determine the question before us.

The Supreme Court has ruled that even nonsectarian prayer during public school graduation ceremonies violates the Establishment Clause because such statements compel students to participate in a religious exercise at the behest of the state. © AP Images/M. Spencer Green.

The principle that government may accommodate the free exercise of religion does not supersede the fundamental limitations imposed by the Establishment Clause. It is beyond dispute that, at a minimum, the Constitution guarantees that government may not coerce anyone to support or participate in religion or its exercise, or otherwise act in a way which "establishes a [state] religion or religious faith, or tends to do so" [*Lynch v. Donnelly* (1984)]. The State's involvement in the school prayers challenged today violates these central principles. . . .

The Issue of Nonsectarian Prayer

We are asked to recognize the existence of a practice of nonsectarian prayer, prayer within the embrace of what is known as the Judeo Christian tradition, prayer which is more acceptable than one which, for example, makes explicit references to the God of Israel, or to Jesus Christ, or to a patron saint. There may be some support, as an empirical observation, to the statement of the Court of Appeals for the Sixth Circuit, picked up by Judge [Levin H.] Campbell's dissent in the Court of Appeals in this case, that there has emerged in this country a civic religion, one which is tolerated when sectarian exercises are not. If common ground can be defined which permits once conflicting faiths to express the shared conviction that there is an ethic and a morality which transcend human invention, the sense of community and purpose sought by all decent societies might be advanced. But though the First Amendment does not allow the government to stifle prayers which aspire to these ends, neither does it permit the government to undertake that task for itself.

The First Amendment's Religion Clauses mean that religious beliefs and religious expression are too precious to be either proscribed or prescribed by the State. The design of the Constitution is that preservation and transmission of religious beliefs and worship is a responsibility and a choice committed to the private sphere, which itself is promised freedom to pursue that mission. It must not be forgotten then, that while concern must be given to define the protection granted to an objector or a dissenting nonbeliever, these same Clauses exist to protect religion from government interference. James Madison, the principal author of the Bill of Rights, did not rest his opposition to a religious establishment on the sole ground of its effect on the minority. A principal ground for his view was: "[E]xperience witnesseth that ecclesiastical establishments, instead of maintaining the purity and efficacy of Religion, have had a contrary operation." . . .

The First Amendment

To endure the speech of false ideas or offensive content and then to counter it is part of learning how to live in a pluralistic society, a society which insists upon open discourse towards the end of a tolerant citizenry. And tolerance presupposes some mutuality of obligation. It is argued that our constitutional vision of a free society requires confidence in our own ability to accept or reject ideas of which we do not approve, and that prayer at a high school graduation does nothing more than offer a choice. By the time they are seniors, high school students no doubt have been required to attend classes and assemblies and to complete assignments exposing them to ideas they find distasteful or immoral or absurd or all of these. Against this background, students may consider it an odd measure of justice to be subjected during the course of their educations to ideas deemed offensive and irreligious, but to be denied a brief, formal prayer ceremony that the school offers in return. This argument cannot prevail, however. It overlooks a fundamental dynamic of the Constitution.

The First Amendment protects speech and religion by quite different mechanisms. Speech is protected by ensuring its full expression even when the government participates, for the very object of some of our most important speech is to persuade the government to adopt an idea as its own. The method for protecting freedom of worship and freedom of conscience in religious matters is quite the reverse. In religious debate or expression the government is not a prime participant, for the Framers deemed religious establishment antithetical to the freedom of all. The Free Exercise Clause embraces a freedom of conscience and worship that has close parallels in the speech provisions of the First Amendment, but the Establishment Clause is a specific prohibition on forms of state intervention in religious affairs with no precise counterpart in the speech provisions. The explanation lies in the lesson of history that was and is the inspiration for the Establishment Clause, the lesson that in the hands of government what might begin as a tolerant expression of religious views may end in a policy to indoctrinate and coerce. A State created orthodoxy puts at grave risk that freedom of belief and conscience, which are the sole assurance that religious faith is real, not imposed.

The lessons of the First Amendment are as urgent in the modern world as in the 18th century when it was written. One timeless lesson is that if citizens are subjected to State-sponsored religious exercises, the State disavows its own duty to guard and respect that sphere of inviolable conscience and belief which is the mark of a free people. To compromise that principle today would be to deny our own tradition and forfeit our standing to urge others to secure the protections of that tradition for themselves.

Freedom of Religion in School

As we have observed before, there are heightened concerns with protecting freedom of conscience from subtle coercive pressure in the elementary and secondary public schools. Our decisions in *Engel v. Vitale* (1962) and *Abington School District* [*v. Schempp* (1963)] recognize, among other things, that prayer exercises in public schools carry a particular risk of indirect coercion. The concern may not be limited to the context of schools, but it is most pronounced there. What to most believers may seem nothing more than a reasonable request that the nonbeliever respect their religious practices, in a school context may appear to the nonbeliever or dissenter to be an attempt to employ the machinery of the State to enforce a religious orthodoxy. . . .

Our society would be less than true to its heritage if it lacked abiding concern for the values of its young people, and we acknowledge the profound belief of adherents to many faiths that there must be a place in the student's life for precepts of a morality higher even than the law we today enforce. We express no hostility to those aspirations, nor would our oath permit us to do so. A relentless and all-pervasive attempt to exclude religion from every aspect of public life could itself become inconsistent with the Constitution. We recognize that, at graduation time and throughout the course of the educational process, there will be instances when religious values, religious practices, and religious persons will have some interaction with the public schools and their students. But these matters, often questions of accommodation of religion, are not before us. The sole question presented is whether a religious exercise may be conducted at a graduation ceremony in circumstances where, as we have found, young graduates who object are induced to conform. No holding by this Court suggests that a school can persuade or compel a student to participate in a religious exercise. That is being done here, and it is forbidden by the Establishment Clause of the First Amendment.

> *"The religious liberty protected by the Constitution is abridged when the State affirmatively sponsors the particular religious practice of prayer."*

Student-Led Prayer at Football Games Violates the First Amendment

The Supreme Court's Decision

John Paul Stevens

In the following viewpoint John Paul Stevens, writing for the majority of the Court, contends that school-sponsored prayer at football games, even if led by students, is contrary to the religious liberty guaranteed by the First Amendment. Whereas the Court emphasizes that nothing can prevent a student from voluntarily praying at school or at a school event, school officials are not allowed to be in the business of sanctioning any student-led school prayer. The Court notes that although the student-led prayer in this case came about by student vote, the will of the majority may not be used to eclipse the First Amendment rights of the minority: The majority of students who want to exercise their freedom of expression of religion by praying at football games may not, by a vote, deny the minority protection from the government establish-

ment of religion through school-sponsored prayer. Stevens served as associate justice of the US Supreme Court from 1975 until his retirement in 2010.

The Santa Fe Independent School District ([referred to here-after as the] District) is a political subdivision of the State of Texas responsible for the education of more than 4,000 students in a small community in the southern part of the State. The District includes the Santa Fe High School, two primary schools, an intermediate school and the junior high school. Respondents are two sets of current or former students and their respective mothers. One family is Mormon and the other is Catholic. The District Court permitted respondents [referred to collectively in the case name as "Doe" and herein as "Does"] to litigate anonymously to protect them from intimidation or harassment.

Respondents commenced this action in April 1995 and moved for a temporary restraining order to prevent the District from violating the Establishment Clause at the imminent graduation exercises. In their complaint the Does alleged that the District had engaged in several proselytizing practices, such as promoting attendance at a Baptist revival meeting, encouraging membership in religious clubs, chastising children who held minority religious beliefs, and distributing Gideon Bibles on school premises. They also alleged that the District allowed students to read Christian invocations and benedictions from the stage at graduation ceremonies, and to deliver overtly Christian prayers over the public address system at home football games.

On May 10, 1995, the District Court entered an interim order addressing a number of different issues. With respect to the impending graduation, the order provided that "non-denominational prayer" consisting of "an invocation and/or benediction" could be presented by a senior student or students selected by members of the graduating class. The text of the prayer was to be determined by the students, without scrutiny or preapproval by school officials. References to particular religious figures "such as

Mohammed, Jesus, Buddha, or the like" would be permitted "as long as the general thrust of the prayer is nonproselytizing."

The Football-Game Prayer Policy

In response to that portion of the order, the District adopted a series of policies over several months dealing with prayer at school functions. The policies enacted in May and July [1995] for graduation ceremonies provided the format for the August and October [1995] policies for football games. The May policy provided:

> The board has chosen to permit the graduating senior class, with the advice and counsel of the senior class principal or designee, to elect by secret ballot to choose whether an invocation and benediction shall be part of the graduation exercise. If so chosen the class shall elect by secret ballot, from a list of student volunteers, students to deliver nonsectarian, nonproselytizing invocations and benedictions for the purpose of solemnizing their graduation ceremonies.

The parties stipulated that after this policy was adopted, "the senior class held an election to determine whether to have an invocation and benediction at the commencement [and that the] class voted, by secret ballot, to include prayer at the high school graduation." In a second vote the class elected two seniors to deliver the invocation and benediction.

In July [1995], the District enacted another policy eliminating the requirement that invocations and benedictions be "nonsectarian and nonproselytising," but also providing that if the District were to be enjoined from enforcing that policy, the May [1995] policy would automatically become effective.

The August [1995] policy, which was titled "Prayer at Football Games," was similar to the July policy for graduations. It also authorized two student elections, the first to determine whether "invocations" should be delivered, and the second to select the spokesperson to deliver them. Like the July policy, it contained two parts, an initial statement that omitted any requirement that the content of the invocation be "nonsectarian and nonproselytising," and a fallback provision that automatically added that limitation if the preferred policy should be enjoined. On August 31, 1995, according to the parties' stipulation, "the district's high school students voted to determine whether a student would deliver prayer at varsity football games. . . . The students chose to allow a student to say a prayer at football games." A week later [September 1995], in a separate election, they selected a student "to deliver the prayer at varsity football games."

The final policy (October [1995] policy) is essentially the same as the August policy, though it omits the word "prayer" from its title, and refers to "messages" and "statements" as well as "invocations." It is the validity of that policy that is before us. . . .

Public and Private Speech

The first Clause in the First Amendment to the Federal Constitution provides that "Congress shall make no law respecting an establishment of religion, or prohibiting the free exercise thereof." The Fourteenth Amendment imposes those substantive limitations on the legislative power of the States and their political subdivisions. In *Lee v. Weisman* (1992), we held that a prayer delivered by a rabbi at a middle school graduation ceremony violated that Clause. Although this case involves student prayer at a different type of school function, our analysis is properly guided by the principles that we endorsed in *Lee*.

As we held in that case:

> The principle that government may accommodate the free exercise of religion does not supersede the fundamental limitations imposed by the Establishment Clause. It is beyond dispute that, at a minimum, the Constitution guarantees that government may not coerce anyone to support or participate in religion or its exercise, or otherwise act in a way which 'establishes a [state] religion or religious faith, or tends to do so'" [quoting *Lynch v. Donnelly* (1984).]

In this case the District first argues that this principle is inapplicable to its October [1995] policy because the messages are private student speech, not public speech. It reminds us that "there is a crucial difference between *government* speech endorsing religion, which the Establishment Clause forbids, and *private* speech endorsing religion, which the Free Speech and Free Exercise Clauses protect" [*Board of Ed. of Westside Community Schools (Dist. 66) v. Mergens* (1990)]. We certainly agree with that distinction, but we are not persuaded that the pregame invocations should be regarded as "private speech."

These invocations are authorized by a government policy and take place on government property at government-sponsored school-related events. Of course, not every message delivered under such circumstances is the government's own. We have held, for example, that an individual's contribution to a government-created forum was not government speech. . . .

The Majority and the Minority

Granting only one student access to the stage at a time does not, of course, necessarily preclude a finding that a school has created a limited public forum. Here, however, Santa Fe's student election system ensures that only those messages deemed "appropriate" under the District's policy may be delivered. That is, the majoritarian process implemented by the District guarantees, by definition, that minority candidates will never prevail and that their view will be effectively silenced.

Recently, in *Board of Regents of Univ. of Wis. System v. Southworth* (2000), we explained why student elections that determine, by majority vote, which expressive activities shall receive or not receive school benefits are constitutionally problematic:

> To the extent the referendum substitutes majority determinations for viewpoint neutrality it would undermine the constitutional protection the program requires. The whole theory of viewpoint neutrality is that minority views are treated with the

same respect as are majority views. Access to a public forum, for instance, does not depend upon majoritarian consent. That principle is controlling here.

Like the student referendum for funding in *Southworth*, this student election does nothing to protect minority views but rather places the students who hold such views at the mercy of the majority. Because "fundamental rights may not [are not allowed to] be submitted to vote; they depend on the outcome of no elections" [*West Virginia Bd. of Ed. v. Barnette* (1943)], the District's elections are insufficient safeguards of diverse student speech.

In *Lee*, the school district made the related argument that its policy of endorsing only "civic or nonsectarian" prayer was acceptable because it minimized the intrusion on the audience as a whole. We rejected that claim by explaining that such a majoritarian policy "does not lessen the offense or isolation to the objectors. At best it narrows their number, at worst increases their sense of isolation and affront." Similarly, while Santa Fe's majoritarian election might ensure that *most* of the students are represented, it does nothing to protect the minority; indeed, it likely serves to intensify their offense.

The School's Entanglement with Religion

Moreover, the District has failed to divorce itself from the religious content in the invocations. It has not succeeded in doing so, either by claiming that its policy is "'one of neutrality rather than endorsement'" or by characterizing the individual student as the "circuit-breaker" in the process. Contrary to the District's repeated assertions that it has adopted a "hands-off" approach to the pregame invocation, the realities of the situation plainly reveal that its policy involves both perceived and actual endorsement of religion. In this case, as we found in *Lee*, the "degree of school involvement" makes it clear that the pregame prayers bear "the imprint of the State and thus put school-age children who objected in an untenable position."

The District has attempted to disentangle itself from the religious messages by developing the two-step student election process. The text of the October [1995] policy, however, exposes the extent of the school's entanglement. The elections take place at all only because the school "board *has chosen to permit* students to deliver a brief invocation and/or message" [emphasis added]. The elections thus "shall" be conducted "by the high school student council" and "[u]pon advice and direction of the high school principal." The decision whether to deliver a message is first made by majority vote of the entire student body, followed by a choice of the speaker in a separate, similar majority election. Even though the particular words used by the speaker are not determined by those votes, the policy mandates that the "statement or invocation" be "consistent with the goals and purposes of this policy," which are "to solemnize the event, to promote good sportsmanship and student safety, and to establish the appropriate environment for the competition."

In addition to involving the school in the selection of the speaker, the policy, by its terms, invites and encourages religious messages. The policy itself states that the purpose of the message is "to solemnize the event." A religious message is the most obvious method of solemnizing an event. Moreover, the requirements that the message "promote good citizenship" and "establish the appropriate environment for competition" further narrow the types of message deemed appropriate, suggesting that a solemn, yet nonreligious, message, such as commentary on United States foreign policy, would be prohibited. Indeed, the only type of message that is expressly endorsed in the text is an "invocation"—a term that primarily describes an appeal for divine assistance. In fact, as used in the past at Santa Fe High School, an "invocation" has always entailed a focused religious message. Thus, the expressed purposes of the policy encourage the selection of a religious message, and that is precisely how the students understand the policy. The results of the elections described in the parties' stipulation make it clear that the students understood that the central question before them was whether prayer should be a part of the pregame ceremony. We recognize the important role that public worship plays in many communities, as well as the sincere desire to include public prayer as a part of various occasions so as to mark those occasions' significance. But such religious activity in public schools, as elsewhere, must comport with the First Amendment.

School Endorsement of Prayer

The actual or perceived endorsement of the message, moreover, is established by factors beyond just the text of the policy. Once the student speaker is selected and the message composed, the invocation is then delivered to a large audience assembled as part of a regularly scheduled, school-sponsored function conducted on school property. The message is broadcast over the school's public address system, which remains subject to the control of school officials. It is fair to assume that the pregame ceremony is clothed in the traditional indicia of school sporting events, which generally include not just the team, but also cheerleaders and band members dressed in uniforms sporting the school name and mascot. The school's name is likely written in large print across the field and on banners and flags. The crowd will certainly include many who display the school colors and insignia on their school T-shirts, jackets, or hats and who may also be waving signs displaying the school name. It is in a setting such as this that "[t]he board has chosen to permit" the elected student to rise and give the "statement or invocation."

In this context the members of the listening audience must perceive the pregame message as a public expression of the views of the majority of the student body delivered with the approval of the school administration. In cases involving state participation in a religious activity, one of the relevant questions is "whether an objective observer, acquainted with the text, legislative his-

Football players at Odessa High School in Odessa, Texas, pray after their game in defiance of rulings against student-led prayer at football games. © Joe Raedle/Newsmakers/Getty Images.

tory, and implementation of the statute, would perceive it as a state endorsement of prayer in public schools" [*Wallace v. Jaffree* (1985) (Justice Sandra Day O'Connor concurring in judgment)]. Regardless of the listener's support for, or objection to, the message, an objective Santa Fe High School student will unquestionably perceive the inevitable pregame prayer as stamped with her school's seal of approval.

The text and history of this policy, moreover, reinforce our objective student's perception that the prayer is, in actuality, encouraged by the school. When a governmental entity professes a secular purpose for an arguably religious policy, the government's characterization is, of course, entitled to some deference. But it is nonetheless the duty of the courts to "distinguis[h] a sham secular purpose from a sincere one." . . .

School sponsorship of a religious message is impermissible because it sends the ancillary message to members of the audience who are nonadherants "that they are outsiders, not full members of the political community, and an accompanying message to adherants that they are insiders, favored members of the political community [*Lynch v. Donnelly* (Justice O'Connor concurring)]. The delivery of such a message—over the school's public address system, by a speaker representing the student body, under the supervision of school faculty, and pursuant to a school policy that explicitly and implicitly encourages public prayer—is not properly characterized as "private" speech.

The Issue of Government Coercion

The District next argues that its football policy is distinguishable from the graduation prayer in *Lee* because it does not coerce students to participate in religious observances. Its argument has two parts: first, that there is no impermissible government coercion because the pregame messages are the product of student choices; and second, that there is really no coercion at all because attendance at an extracurricular event, unlike a graduation ceremony, is voluntary.

The reasons just discussed explaining why the alleged "circuit-breaker" mechanism of the dual elections and student speaker do not turn public speech into private speech also demonstrate why these mechanisms do not insulate the school from the coercive element of the final message. . . .

Even if we regard every high school student's decision to attend a home football game as purely voluntary, we are nevertheless persuaded that the delivery of a pregame prayer has the improper effect of coercing those present to participate in an act of religious worship. For "the government may no more use social pressure to enforce orthodoxy than it may use more direct means." As in *Lee*, "[w]hat to most believers may seem nothing more than a reasonable request that the nonbeliever respect their religious practices, in a school context may appear to the nonbeliever or dissenter to be an attempt to employ the machinery of the State to enforce a religious orthodoxy." The constitutional command will not permit the District "to exact religious conformity from a student as the price" of joining her classmates at a varsity football game.

The Religion Clauses of the First Amendment prevent the government from making any law respecting the establishment of religion or prohibiting the free exercise thereof. By no means do these commands impose a prohibition on all religious activity in our public schools. Indeed, the common purpose of the Religion Clauses "is to secure religious liberty" [*Engel v. Vitale* (1962)]. Thus, nothing in the Constitution as interpreted by this Court prohibits any public school student from voluntarily praying at any time before, during, or after the school day. But the religious liberty protected by the Constitution is abridged when the State affirmatively sponsors the particular religious practice of prayer.

> "Neither side in this debate wants speech to be really free when it comes to religion."

Court Decisions and Public Opinion Illustrate the Conflict Between Freedom of Speech and Freedom of Religion

Cathy Young

In the following viewpoint Cathy Young argues that court cases illustrate that the First Amendment's guarantees of freedom of speech and freedom from the government establishment of religion are often in conflict. Young claims that the US Supreme Court's decision in Santa Fe Independent School District v. Doe *(2000), disallowing school-endorsed student-led prayer at football games, illustrates this conflict. Young contends that in several other cases involving the place of religion at school, religious student speech seems to be unfairly singled out as unprotected by the First Amendment. Nonetheless, Young notes that those in favor of more freedom of religious speech do not necessarily want absolute freedom, often singling out the topic of religion as deserving of less freedom of expression. Young is a contributing editor at* Reason *magazine and Reason.com.*

Cathy Young, "God Talk: The First Amendment vs. Freedom of Speech," *Reason,* vol. 32, January 2001, pp. 37–40. Reproduced by permission.

The latest round in the perennial legal battle over the separation of church and state ended on June 19 [2000], when the U.S. Supreme Court struck down a Texas school district's policy permitting voluntary, student-initiated public prayers before high school football games. But the litigation over religious expression in public schools is likely to continue. It is a conflict in which two key First Amendment protections—freedom of speech and the prohibition against state establishment of religion—seem to collide. And yet the real paradox, perhaps, is that neither side in this debate wants speech to be *really* free when it comes to religion.

The Issue of Student-Initiated Religious Expression

The Supreme Court case *Santa Fe Independent School District v. Doe*, began in 1995 when several families challenged the practice of having a prayer delivered over the school's public address system at the start of each home varsity football game. The plaintiffs—not atheists but Catholics and Mormons—saw this as part of a general pattern of promotion of a specific brand of Christianity by the schools of the mostly Baptist town. Teachers led prayers before lunch, handed out flyers for revival meetings, and in some cases actively proselytized students of other faiths and disparaged their beliefs.

After the lawsuit was filed, the district took steps to curb these excesses and devised an ostensibly neutral solution to the problem of public prayer at football games: The students would elect a speaker to deliver pre-game remarks—religious or secular—to "solemnize the event." It is this policy that the high court has rejected as thinly disguised public sponsorship of prayer.

In a caustic dissent, Chief Justice William Rehnquist complained that the majority opinion, written by Justice John Paul Stevens, "bristles with hostility to all things religious in public life." Yet Rehnquist conceded that if the disputed policy resulted in prayer, say, 90 percent of the time, it would probably be unconstitutional.

Conservative critics of a strict separation of church and state frame the issue as one of free speech and free exercise of religion. This emphasis is shrewd political strategy—no one wants to admit to being against either freedom—but it also raises a thorny issue. If government schools allow student-initiated religious expression at official school events, are they unconstitutionally promoting religion? If they muzzle such expression, are they unconstitutionally suppressing speech?

The Treatment of Religious Speech

Even conservative Pepperdine University law professor Douglas Kmiec, who believes that modern secularism has "perverted" the constitutional ban on an official state religion into a mandate to banish religiosity from the public square, wrote in *The Wall Street Journal* that, "given the peculiar facts of the case, the Supreme Court may have been right" to strike down the Santa Fe policy. Those facts included the district's history of practices that were clearly unconstitutional even under the narrowest interpretation of the Establishment Clause. The policy allowing an elected student speaker to deliver an invocation was rather transparently designed as a way to preserve pre-game prayer.

But in other, more complex cases currently moving through the legal system, there is a far stronger claim that absolute separation unfairly singles out religious speech. Take the saga of the brothers Chris and Jason Niemeyer, devout evangelical Christians and successive class valedictorians at Oroville High School in California in 1998 and 1999. The Niemeyers were barred from giving the traditional commencement address to their classmates because they wanted to talk about their faith.

As many schools require, Chris Niemeyer gave the school administrators an advance copy of his speech, which asserted that all people are "God's children, through Jesus Christ's death, when we accept his free love and saving grace," and urged listeners to embrace a "personal relationship" with God. The principal told him to tone down the religious message. After an unsuccessful attempt to get a court order securing his right to speak, the boy wanted to make brief remarks at graduation explaining why he couldn't give a speech. But school officials stopped him on his way to the podium and told him he couldn't speak at all—a gesture that prompted loud protests from the crowd and nearly sparked a riot.

The following year, Jason Niemeyer submitted a valedictory address that, while less focused on religion, concluded by urging all those present "to take advantage of the friendship that is offered us in Christ." After consulting with attorneys, the school forbade him to give the speech and also nixed a revised version with no direct references to Jesus.

Both of the brothers are suing the school district. So far, the courts have sided with the school, which argues that graduation is an extension of the school curriculum and that, therefore, sectarian commencement messages should not be permitted.

The Establishment of Religion

Yet had the brothers been allowed to speak, interpreting their remarks as "establishment of religion" by the state would have been far more of a stretch than in the Texas football case. A valedictorian's address has a clear secular purpose, and neither boy would have been the sole graduation speaker. It is doubtful that any student in the audience could have perceived a religiously themed valedictory speech as official endorsement of a sectarian creed by the school (any more than Chris Niemeyer's election as class president in his senior year, at a time when he was also the co-leader of a Christian club at school, amounted to an endorsement of religion).

To remove any shade of suspicion, an administrator could have made a statement that any expressions of religious faith reflected the speakers' individual beliefs. Indeed, the concern of the officials seems to have been less that some people would feel coerced or discriminated against than that some people would feel uncomfortable.

"Honest! When I said 'Jesus Christ,' I was *swearing,* not *praying!"*

"Honest! When I said 'Jesus Christ' I was swearing, not praying!" by Rex May-Baloo, www .CartoonStock.com.

In a declaration filed in the legal case, Chris Niemeyer's co-valedictorian, Delisa Freistadt, who is Jewish, stated that she was glad the court didn't "force" her to listen to his speech. The Niemeyers' attorneys counter, rather persuasively, that it is part of the American way that we are sometimes forced to listen to speech we don't like. (Freistadt could have countered speech with more speech and used her time at the podium to talk about respecting religious differences.) As applied in this case so far, the First Amendment seems to be less a guarantee of religious freedom than a speech code guaranteeing that no one's feelings are hurt.

A Possible Double Standard

There may be an anti-religion double standard at work as well. Some of the Niemeyers' local supporters gripe that the same school officials who muzzled the boys allowed the installation of a Vietnam War mural many people found objectionable. It also seems likely that if a public school had silenced a vale-dictorian who wanted to praise vegetarianism or assail racism, the mainstream media and the American Civil Liberties Union [ACLU] would have blasted the decision as an outrageous act of censorship.

The ACLU has criticized the free speech defense of student-initiated prayer at graduation, cautioning that such a position would force schools to grant equal access to all speakers of all viewpoints on a first come, first served basis—a less relevant concern when the issue is one of free expression for speakers already chosen on an ideologically neutral basis. It is also worth noting that the Colorado ACLU has championed the right of black students to wear a ceremonial African cloth over their graduation gowns as a protected form of expression.

An even better case that strict separationism can turn into censorship can be made in a suit currently pending in the U.S. Court of Appeals for the 3rd Circuit in Philadelphia, brought by the parents of Medford, New Jersey, schoolboy Zachary Hood. In 1996, each child in the boy's first-grade public school class was asked to choose a story to read aloud. Zachary's selection, the story of the reconciliation between the brothers Jacob and Esau from *The Beginner's Bible*, was deemed inappropriate by the teacher, even though it contained no mention of God or miracles. He was told that he could read it to her in private but not to the entire class.

In 1999 a three-judge panel of the 3rd Circuit ruled that the teacher acted properly, agreeing with the school's rather wobbly argument that permitting the story to be read in the classroom would have sent a message to the impressionable kiddies that "the teacher or the school endorsed the Bible." Late last year, however, the full [appeals] court vacated that decision and agreed to consider the case, which may go all the way to the Supreme Court [the Court declined to hear the case].

The Religious Viewpoint

It would be difficult to dispute . . . religious conservatives' claim that the treatment of Zachary Hood or of the Niemeyers reflects "viewpoint discrimination" against religious speech. It is fairly clear that in these instances it is the exclusion rather than the inclusion of religion that may "discriminate against, or oppress, a particular sect or religion," as Justice William Brennan put it in the 1963 ruling *School District of Abington v. Schempp*, which found mandatory school prayer unconstitutional.

But it would also be disingenuous for the anti-secularists to claim that they want religion to be treated as just another viewpoint in the marketplace of ideas—a viewpoint which can be defended but can also be attacked and even ridiculed, like any other idea. Indeed, the same people who wax poetic about defending religious liberty for Christians can get very unhappy with the wrong kind of speech about religion. Just as religious conservatives now couch their demands for prayer in public schools in the "liberal" language of free speech, their attempts to squelch what used to be called sacrilege are couched in the politically correct language of anti-bigotry and opposition to "hate speech." The charge of "Christian bashing" (or "Catholic bashing") has been directed, for instance, at the ABC [TV] show *Nothing Sacred*, which questioned Catholic doctrine on birth control and priestly celibacy.

In 1998 news of a Broadway production of Terrence McNally's play *Corpus Christi*, depicting a gay Jesus-like character, sparked a predictable firestorm. The Catholic League for Religious and Civil Rights launched a letter-writing campaign demanding that the production be canceled. It is true, of course, that a protest is not censorship. But when the Manhattan Theater Club decided to cancel the play due to threats of violence and arson, the Catholic League's jubilant reaction did not show a strong commitment to free speech. While formally deploring the threats, the league warned that if another company picked up *Corpus Christi*, [the league] would "wage a war that no one will forget." (The theater

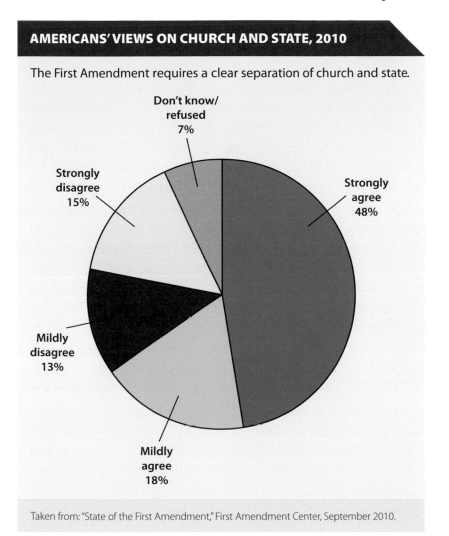

AMERICANS' VIEWS ON CHURCH AND STATE, 2010

The First Amendment requires a clear separation of church and state.

Don't know/
refused
7%

Strongly
disagree
15%

Strongly
agree
48%

Mildly
disagree
13%

Mildly
agree
18%

Taken from: "State of the First Amendment," First Amendment Center, September 2010.

eventually revived the production after coming under fire from the press and from authors.) Catholic League President William Donohue explicitly, and favorably, compared the anti-*Corpus Christi* protests to the actions taken by racial, ethnic, and feminist groups against speech they find offensive.

And in July [2000], in what may be the most creative use of hate speech phraseology to date, L. Brent Bozell's Media Research

Center ran an ad accusing CBS of "condoning religious bigotry." *Early Show* host Bryant Gumbel had been caught on camera saying "What a f---ing idiot!" after an interview with the Family Research Council's Robert Knight, who had defended on religious grounds the Boy Scouts' exclusion of gays. Even if Gumbel was referring to Knight and not, as some have claimed, to a CBS staffer, it is noteworthy that he used no slurs referring to Knight's faith. (Is it racist to call Al Sharpton a f---ing idiot?) Nonetheless, Bozell invoked CBS' firing of sports oddsmaker Jimmy "The Greek" Snyder for televised comments about the innate racial superiority of black athletes and concluded that "racial bigotry on CBS is dealt with unequivocally; religious bigotry on CBS is met with a disinterested yawn."

The Separation Between Church and State

In an essay published in *The New York Times Magazine* last January [2000], legal commentator Jeffrey Rosen noted that the strict separationism endorsed by the courts in the early 1970s, which held that the government could not support any religious activity in any form, has given way to "a very different constitutional principle that demands equal treatment for religion." Under this doctrine, Bible study clubs and prayer groups can function on public school property on a par with other student groups, and parochial schools can receive federal aid for special education programs on a par with other schools. (School vouchers that would subsidize tuition at religious schools remain a more contentious issue.)

Rosen insightfully links the crumbling of the wall between church and state to the rise of cultural diversity: "In an era when religious identity now competes with race, sex and ethnicity as a central aspect of how Americans define themselves, it seems like discrimination—the only unforgivable sin in a multicultural age—to forbid people to express their religious beliefs in an increasingly fractured public sphere." As Rosen concludes, the resulting expansion of freedom of religious expression may well be a healthy development for public life. But the examples of race and sex also point to certain dangers. While the new appreciation of diversity can liberate discussion and expression, it can just as easily narrow the range of acceptable speech in order to protect sensitivities.

| "*Justice Kennedy and seven of his colleagues need a renewal of their understanding of the First Amendment in our history.*"

The Supreme Court Has Gone Too Far in Limiting Student Religious Speech

Nat Hentoff

In the following viewpoint Nat Hentoff argues that the US Supreme Court is not doing its job of upholding the First Amendment rights of students. Hentoff contends that in lower court cases that the Supreme Court refused to hear, student rights to free expression were violated. In both cases, he says, their rights were violated because the content of their expression had a religious component. Hentoff claims that there is no constitutional right to not be offended by what others say, even in a public school setting. Thus, he concludes that the First Amendment rights of students need to be protected by the Court, even when their speech makes others uncomfortable. Hentoff is a senior fellow at the Cato Institute and author of The War on the Bill of Rights and the Gathering Resistance.

Nat Hentoff, "Free Religious Speech for Students in School?" Cato.org, April 12, 2010. Reproduced by permission.

L ike [Thomas] Jefferson and [James] Madison, I strongly believe in separation of church and state. And if a principal
were to mandate school-directed prayer in classrooms, then
that would be a violation of that separation. However, if at commencement, a valedictorian speaks of what God and Christ
have meant to her life, that is her First Amendment right to free
speech! The [Chief Justice John] Roberts Supreme Court does
not appear to agree.

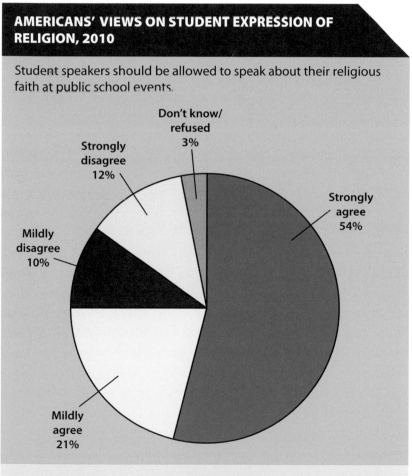

**AMERICANS' VIEWS ON STUDENT EXPRESSION OF
RELIGION, 2010**

Student speakers should be allowed to speak about their religious
faith at public school events.

Don't know/
refused
3%

Strongly
disagree
12%

Strongly
agree
54%

Mildly
disagree
10%

Mildly
agree
21%

Taken from: "State of the First Amendment," First Amendment Center, September 2010.

Lindsay Pease, right, and her mother, Jan, read the Bible at their home in Columbus, Georgia. Pease feels that schools have moved too far from an understanding of religion. © AP Images/ John Bazemore.

A Valedictorian's Free-Speech Rights

Last November [2009], the Supreme Court refused to hear an appeal by Brittany McComb, who—as a 2006 valedictorian at Foothill High School in Nevada—had her microphone cut off by school officials when she started to speak about how God and Christ had taught her to experience something greater than herself, inspiring her to rise above her early high school failures.

Brittany had been forewarned. Her high school required a prior draft copy of commencement speeches and censored all references in hers to her religious faith. She went ahead anyway because, as a student of the First Amendment, she knew she was speaking as an individual—and not on behalf of the state as represented by officials of her public high school.

With the help of the Rutherford Institute, headed by John Whitehead—a premier protector of all rights in the Bill of Rights—Brittany appealed the literal cutting off of her First Amendment rights [*Brittany McComb v. Gretchen Crehan* (2006)].

The "liberal" 9th U.S. Circuit Court of Appeals supported the school's censorship because she was "proselytizing." But Brittany was speaking for, and about, herself. She was not trying to convert anyone.

When I often write that the Constitution is my only Bible, I'm telling the reader where I'm coming from—not that he or she should join me as a non-believer in God. I'm not proselytizing either.

Brittany's appeal came to the Supreme Court, which refused to hear it. There was no written dissent by any of the Roberts' Court justices.

Thomas Jefferson, in his *Notes on the State of Virginia* (1782), emphasized that the government has no authority over the natural rights of conscience: "The legitimate powers of government extend only to such acts as are injurious to others. But it does me no injury for my neighbor to say there are twenty gods, or no god. It neither picks my pocket nor breaks my leg."

The censored Brittany McComb did not injure anyone, but her public high school unconstitutionally deeply injured her free-speech rights—an injury in which the Supreme Court has become complicit.

Political Correctness Goes Too Far

Here is another case that came before the Supreme Court in March [2010]. At the Henry M. Jackson High School in Snohomish County, state of Washington, the senior members of the school's woodwind ensemble are allowed to choose a song from their repertoire to perform at graduation ceremonies. In 2006, they unanimously chose "Ave Maria"—in a purely instrumental performance, with no lyrics.

The superintendent of schools refused to permit the performance because "Ave Maria" is religious in nature and its presence might have offended members of the audience. Welcome to Political Correctness (a.k.a.: Discarding Free Speech) 101.

Kathryn Nurre, a member of the school's wind ensemble, fully aware that school authorities had violated her free-speech rights, contacted First Amendment warrior John Whitehead and the Rutherford Institute. In September 2009, the "liberal" 9th U.S. Circuit Court of Appeals again upheld the censoring school system's invoking [of a] a right that cannot be found anywhere in the Constitution—the "right" not to be offended.

Dissenting Judge Milan D. Smith declared that "if the majority's reasoning on this issue becomes widely adopted, the practical effect will be for public school administrators to chill—or even kill—musical and artistic presentations by their students in school-sponsored limited public fora [spaces] where those presentations contain any trace of religious inspiration, for fear of criticism by a member of the public, however extreme that person's views may be. The First Amendment neither requires nor condones such a result."

When I first heard of this case, *Nurre v. (Superintendent Carol) Whitehead* [2009], I was sure that at least the requisite four members of the Supreme Court would vote to hear Nurre's appeal. But John Paul Stevens, Ruth Bader Ginsburg, Stephen Breyer, Anthony Kennedy, Antonin Scalia, Clarence Thomas (who has a sound record on the First Amendment), Sonia Sotomayor and Chief Justice John Roberts were silent.

The only dissenter from the "conservative" Roberts Supreme Court's refusal to even hear *Nurre v. Whitehead* was Justice Samuel Alito, who channeled Jefferson and Madison, saying:

> When a public school purports to allow students to express themselves, it must respect the students' free speech rights. School administrators [are not allowed to] behave like puppet masters who create the illusion that students are engaging in

personal expression when in fact the school administration is pulling the strings.

The Supreme Court and the First Amendment

I was greatly heartened when, after the fear generated by 9/11 led to government assaults on the Bill of Rights, Justice Anthony Kennedy went to a number of high schools to warn that "The Constitution needs renewal and understanding each generation, or it's not going to last."

With regard to the First Amendment, from which all our individual liberties against government flow, Justice Kennedy and seven of his colleagues need a renewal of their understanding of the First Amendment in our history—including its vital role in teaching students why they are Americans.

I'm sure Kathryn Nurre would be glad to assist the eight justices in their remedial education. Meanwhile, in how many public school civics classes will *Nurre v. Whitehead* and *McComb v. Crehan* be discussed? I'm not optimistic.

And where is former constitutional law professor [and US president] Barack Obama? He is also among the silent. And where was the ACLU [American Civil Liberties Union] in these two denials of who we are as Americans? John Whitehead deserves the ACLU's Medal of Liberty.

| "The separation of church and state will never be fully respected in public schools if we aren't vigilant."

Students Need to Speak Out Against Religion in Public Schools

Rob Boston

In the following viewpoint Rob Boston contends that the recent experience of a public school student shows that people in the United States need to be more vigilant about keeping religion out of public schools. Boston recounts how a public high school student spoke out against the religious preaching of his history teacher. Boston laments what he deems an inadequate response by the school, and warns people that this kind of incident is not an isolated one. He encourages students to speak out against violations of the First Amendment and urges others to support the students who do so. Boston is the assistant director of communications for Americans United for Separation of Church and State, a nonprofit educational organization.

Rob Boston, "Putting an End to 'Teacher-Preachers' in Public Schools," *Humanist,* vol. 67, May–June 2007, pp. 38–39. Reproduced by permission of the author.

Recently [fall 2006] a public high school teacher stood before his class and told the students that if they didn't accept Jesus Christ as their personal savior, they would go to hell. Furthermore, he added that evolution is a crock and dinosaurs lived on Noah's ark.

Your first thought might be, where did this happen—Mississippi or rural Texas?

Try New Jersey—ten miles outside of New York City.

A Student Speaks Up

Matthew LaClair, a junior at Kearny High School in Kearny, New Jersey, grew frustrated when David Paszkiewicz, instructor of an honors history course, began veering off topic and delivering sermons. But LaClair didn't want to complain to school officials before he had proof, so he secretly taped Paszkiewicz's preaching.

"If you reject his gift of salvation, then you know where you belong," Paszkiewicz is heard saying on the tape. "He did everything in his power to make sure that you could go to heaven, so much so that he took your sins on his own body, suffered your pains for you, and he's saying, 'Please, accept me, believe.' If you reject that, you belong in hell."

Confronted with the tape, Paszkiewicz wasn't able to deny that he was preaching. He's now claiming he was set up by LaClair. If Paszkiewicz is to be believed, LaClair somehow tricked him into proselytizing as part of a plot to get the teacher in trouble. He has yet to explain exactly how or why LaClair might have done this.

The School's Response

Kearny school officials reacted to the flap in a most curious way. They claimed they would rein in Paszkiewicz, but to date most of their punitive actions have been directed at LaClair. The school system implemented a new policy barring students from secretly taping lectures, and they dispersed that particular history class, sending LaClair and his classmates off to other teachers.

The decision to break up the class has made LaClair less than popular. Apparently Paszkiewicz is a well-liked teacher, and some students are mad about being forced out of his class. Others accept Paszkiewicz's rather implausible version of events. LaClair has been ostracized, taunted, and even received a death threat.

LaClair's parents are insisting that the school protect their son; they are also considering legal action. At a recent meeting of the school board, LaClair said, "During the whole time I've been harassed and bullied, you've done nothing to defend me; you make it look like I've done something wrong."

The sad incident is a reminder that the religious neutrality of the U.S. public school system is never truly secure. It's remarkable and quite sad that incidents like this still occur forty-five years after the U.S. Supreme Court banned mandatory, school-sponsored devotional exercises.

Religion in Public Schools

What's worse is that the Kearny flap isn't an isolated example. Every year attorneys at Americans United for Separation of

 An Uncontroversial Principle

A public school's approach to religion must have a legitimate educational purpose, not a devotional one. Public schools should not be in the business of preaching to students or trying to persuade them to adopt certain religious beliefs. Parents, not school officials, are responsible for overseeing a young person's religious upbringing. This is not a controversial principle. In fact, most parents would demand these basic rights.

Americans United for Separation of Church and State, "Prayer and the Public Schools: Religion, Education, and Your Rights," no date. www.au.org

Church and State receive dozens of complaints about inappropriate forms of religion in public schools. Examples range from school-sponsored prayer at mandatory assemblies and in-school Bible distribution by Gideons [a group of evangelical Christians] to efforts to teach creationism and adopt Bible classes that reflect fundamentalist dogma.

For many years religious right leaders have talked openly about abandoning the secular public school system, which they believe to be damned. One ambitious group formed in 1997 called itself "Exodus 2000," hoping that all fundamentalist parents would remove their children from public schools within three years.

It didn't happen. Despite all the talk about the growth of private education and home schooling, the fact is that public education serves 90 percent of U.S. children. That number has remained constant for many years, and it's a figure that excites other factions of the religious right. Rather than abandon public schools, leaders of this group see public schools—and the captive audiences therein—as plump targets for evangelism.

This "stealth evangelism" takes many forms. Americans United regularly receives complaints about groups offering free assemblies to public schools. The event usually either turns into a sermon or students are pressured to attend a "party" later that evening that is really a revival service at a local church. (A tip for school officials: be wary of free assemblies, especially when the group offering them has the word "ministry" appended to its name. Even if an organization disguises its true intent, a few minutes of research on the Web can usually smoke out the proselytizers.)

Preaching teachers are more problematic because sometimes they fly under the radar, offering in-class sermons without the sanction or knowledge of school officials. Many young people look at teachers as authority figures and are reluctant to challenge them in class. Others fear the type of ostracism and harassment that LaClair is undergoing.

The Americans United for the Separation of Church and State filed a lawsuit in 2006 to have this portrait of Jesus removed from the hallway of Bridgeport High School in Bridgeport, West Virginia. The organization receives dozens of complaints every year about religious practice in public schools. © AP Images/Bob Shaw.

Legitimate Instruction and Sectarian Dogma

In Paszkiewicz's case, his stunt was doubly offensive. The threats of hellfire were bad enough, and the promotion of creationism only made things worse. One can only wonder what the school's science faculty thinks about a history teacher's decision to push pseudo-science in class. And how long would Paszkiewicz have gotten away with any of this had he been a Muslim, a humanist, or even a Jehovah's Witness?

Legitimate instruction about religion as an academic subject in public schools isn't a problem. As long as it's done in a non-dogmatic manner intended to educate, not indoctrinate, such instruction can be a valuable addition to the curriculum.

The introduction of sectarian dogma is something else entirely. Not only is it unconstitutional, it's just plain rude. What Paszkiewicz essentially told all of the Jews, atheists, Buddhists, and mainline Christians in his class was: The religion or moral philosophy your parents chose to raise you with is wrong; I know better than they do, and you should discard your family's religion in favor of my alternative.

So much for parental rights.

The Need for Vigilance

Public education officials in Kearny have some work to do. First, they need to apologize to LaClair and his family and make sure the harassment stops. Then they need to rein in Paszkiewicz.

All of us have a job, too. The separation of church and state will never be fully respected in public schools if we aren't vigilant. We must never assume that this issue is settled. The law has been on our side for nearly fifty years, yet we still find ourselves fighting attempts to inject sectarianism into our public schools.

One of the most important things we can do is support those who are willing to stick their necks out in defense of liberty. Disputes over religion in public schools bring out the worst in some people. Ironically, it is often the "holier-than-thou" brigade that is the first to weigh in with verbal abuse, threats, and intimidation.

If the people who oppose the religious right's attempt to "Christianize" our public schools feel isolated and scorned, they might take a pass the next time a violation occurs. We need to work to create an atmosphere where whistleblowers like Matthew LaClair are treated like heroes, not villains, for speaking out for their constitutional rights.

Organizations to Contact

The editors have compiled the following list of organizations concerned with the issues debated in this book. The descriptions are derived from materials provided by the organizations.

Alliance Defense Fund (ADF)

15100 N 90th Street, Scottsdale, AZ 85260

(480) 444-0020 • fax (480) 444-0028

website: www.alliancedefensefund.org

ADF is a Christian organization that works to defend religious freedom. The organization provides legal defense for cases involving religious freedom, the sanctity of life, marriage, and the family. ADF publishes books, brochures, and pamphlets, which include "The Truth About Student Rights."

American Center for Law and Justice (ACLJ)

PO Box 90555, Washington, DC 20090-0555

(800) 296-4529

website: www.aclj.org

ACLJ is dedicated to protecting religious and constitutional freedoms. It has participated in numerous cases before the Supreme Court, Federal Court of Appeals, Federal District Courts, and various state courts regarding freedom of religion and freedom of speech. At its website ACLJ has numerous memos and position papers available, including "Protecting the Rights of Students."

American Civil Liberties Union (ACLU)

125 Broad Street, 18th Floor, New York, NY 10004

(212) 549-2500

e-mail: infoaclu@aclu.org

website: www.aclu.org

The ACLU is a national organization that works to defend Americans' civil rights as guaranteed in the US Constitution. The organization works in courts, legislatures, and communities to defend First Amendment rights, the right to equal protection, the right to due process, and the right to privacy. The ACLU publishes the newsletter *Civil Liberties Alert*, as well as other publications, including "Reclaiming Our Rights: Declaration of First Amendment Rights and Grievances."

American Jewish Congress

115 East 57th Street, Suite 11, New York, NY 10022
(212) 879-4500 • fax (212) 758-1633
e-mail: contact@ajcongress.org
website: www.ajcongress.org

The American Jewish Congress is an association of Jewish Americans organized to defend Jewish interests at home and abroad. The association engages in public policy advocacy—using diplomacy, legislation, and the courts—to defend religious freedom in the United States. The American Jewish Congress has several publications available at its website, including "Religion and the Public Schools: A Summary of the Law."

Americans United for Separation of Church and State

1301 K Street NW, Suite 850, East Tower, Washington, DC 20005
(202) 466-3234 • fax (202) 466-2587
e-mail: americansunited@au.org
website: www.au.org

Americans United for Separation of Church and State is a non-profit educational organization dedicated to preserving the constitutional principle of church-state separation. The organization works to defend religious liberty in Congress and state legislatures, and it aims to ensure new legislation and policy protects church-state separation. Americans United for Separation of

Church and State publishes several books and pamphlets, including *Religion in the Public Schools: A Road Map for Avoiding Lawsuits and Respecting Parents' Legal Rights.*

The Becket Fund for Religious Liberty
3000 K Street NW, Suite 220, Washington, DC 20007
(202) 955-0095 • fax (202) 955-0090
website: www.becketfund.org

The Becket Fund for Religious Liberty is a public-interest law firm protecting the free expression of all religious traditions. The firm operates in three arenas: the courts of law (litigation), the court of public opinion (media), and the academy (scholarship). At its website, the Becket Fund has information about cases in which it has participated, which include cases aimed at protecting private religious schools from discrimination and aimed at preserving a legitimate role for religious discourse and expression in public schools.

First Freedom Center
1321 E Main Street, Richmond, VA 23219-3629
(804) 643-1786 • fax (804) 644-5024
e-mail: caff@firstfreedom.org
website: www.firstfreedom.org

The First Freedom Center is a nonprofit, nondenominational, educational organization committed to advancing the fundamental human rights of freedom of religion and freedom of conscience. At its Richmond, Virginia, headquarters the First Freedom Center provides exhibits and programs that examine America's progress in striving for religious freedom. At its website, the First Freedom Center has a variety of historical documents on religious freedom, as well as online exhibits related to religious freedom.

Foundation for Moral Law
PO Box 4086, Montgomery, AL 36103-4086

(334) 262-1245 • fax (334) 262-1708
e-mail: info@morallaw.org
website: www.morallaw.org

The Foundation for Moral Law is a nonprofit organization that aims to restore the knowledge of God in law and government. The organization represents individuals involved in religious liberties cases, and conducts educational seminars on the importance of God in law and government. At its website, the Foundation for Moral Law has information about cases in which it has participated, including *amicus curiae* (friend of the court) briefs filed in cases involving bibles in schools, a moment of silence in schools, and other issues related to teen religious rights.

Freedom Forum

555 Pennsylvania Ave. NW, Washington, DC 20001
(202) 292-6100
e-mail: news@freedomforum.org
website: www.freedomforum.org

The Freedom Forum is a nonpartisan foundation dedicated to free press, free speech, and free spirit for all people. The forum's First Amendment Center (www.firstamendmentcenter.org) works to preserve and protect First Amendment freedoms through information and education. It publishes an annual report, "State of the First Amendment," as well as numerous publications, including *The Bible and Public Schools: A First Amendment Guide.*

Interfaith Alliance

1212 New York Ave. NW, Suite 1250, Washington, DC 20005
(800) 510-0969 • fax (202) 238-3301
website: www.interfaithalliance.org

The Interfaith Alliance is a national interfaith organization dedicated to protecting the integrity of both religion and democracy in America. The organization celebrates religious freedom by championing individual rights, promoting policies that protect both religion and democracy, and uniting diverse voices to challenge extremism. The Interfaith Alliance publishes a quarterly online newsletter and produces a weekly radio show, *State of Belief*, with podcasts available at its website.

National Youth Rights Association (NYRA)

1101 15th Street NW, Suite 200, Washington, DC, 20005

(202) 835-1739

website: www.youthrights.org

NYRA is a youth-led national nonprofit organization dedicated to fighting for the civil rights and liberties of young people. NYRA has more than 7,000 members representing all 50 states. It seeks to lower the voting age, lower the drinking age, repeal curfew laws, and protect student rights.

People for the American Way (PFAW)

2000 M Street NW, Suite 400, Washington, DC 20036

(202) 467-4999

website: www.pfaw.org

PFAW is an organization that fights for progressive values: equal rights, freedom of speech, religious liberty, and equal justice under the law for every American. The organization works to build and nurture communities of support for its values, and to equip those communities to promote progressive policies, elect progressive candidates, and hold public officials accountable. Among its publications is the report "Back to School with the Religious Right."

Rutherford Institute

PO Box 7482, Charlottesville, VA 22906-7482

(434) 978-3888 • fax (434) 978-1789

e-mail: staff@rutherford.org

website: www.rutherford.org

The Rutherford Institute is a civil liberties organization. It provides legal services in the defense of religious and civil liberties, and it aims to educate members of the public on important issues affecting their constitutional freedoms. The Rutherford Institute publishes commentary, articles, and books, including "The Future Looks Bleak for the First Amendment."

For Further Reading

Books

Bruce J. Dierenfield, *The Battle over School Prayer: How Engel v. Vitale Changed America*. Lawrence: University Press of Kansas, 2007.

Noah Feldman, *Divided by God: America's Church-State Problem—and What We Should Do About It*. New York: Farrar, Straus, and Giroux, 2006.

Kent Greenawalt, *Does God Belong in Public Schools?* Princeton, NJ: Princeton University Press, 2005.

Philip Hamburger, *Separation of Church and State*. Cambridge, MA: Harvard University Press, 2002.

Charles C. Haynes, Sam Chaltain, and Susan M. Glisson, *First Freedoms: A Documentary History of First Amendment Rights in America*. New York: Oxford University Press, 2006.

Robert Kunzman, *Grappling with the Good: Talking About Religion and Morality in Public Schools*. Albany, NY: State University of New York Press, 2006.

Frank Lambert, *The Founding Fathers and the Place of Religion in America*. Princeton, NJ: Princeton University Press, 2003.

Anthony Lewis, *Freedom for the Thought That We Hate: A Biography of the First Amendment*. New York: MJF Books, 2011.

Warren A. Nord, *Does God Make a Difference? Taking Religion Seriously in Our Schools and Universities*. New York: Oxford University Press, 2010.

Stephen D. Solomon, *Ellery's Protest: How One Young Man Defied Tradition and Sparked the Battle over School Prayer*. Ann Arbor: University of Michigan Press, 2009.

R. Murray Thomas, *God in the Classroom: Religion and America's Public Schools*. Westport, CT: Praeger, 2007.

Periodicals and Internet Sources

American Jewish Congress, "Religion and the Public Schools: A Summary of the Law," August 2009. www.ajcongress.org.

Americans United for Separation of Church and State, "First Amendment Fumble: Football Coaches Must Obey School Prayer Law," *Church & State*, April 2009.

Tom Bennett and George Foldesy, "'Our Father in Heaven': A Legal Analysis of the Recitation of the Lord's Prayer by Public School Coaches," *The Clearing House*, March–April 2008.

Robert H. Bork, "What to Do About the First Amendment," *Commentary*, February 1995.

Rob Boston, "First Amendment TOUCHDOWN!" *Church & State*, 2000.

Christianity Today, "Caesar's Sectarians: The Government Keeps Trying to Favor One Kind of Religion Over Another," September 2008.

Current Events, a Weekly Reader Publication, "Reading, Writing, and Religion? A Debate of Biblical Proportions," March 4, 2005.

Thomas Curry, "Separation Anxiety: Church, State, and the Survival of Catholic Schools," *America*, November 22, 2010.

John Eidsmoe, "The War on Christmas," *New American*, December 22, 2008.

C. Welton Gaddy, "Religious Freedom and Church-State Separation," *Human Rights*, Fall 2008.

Allen D. Hertzke, "The Supreme Court and Religious Liberty," *Weekly Standard*, October 18, 2010.

Susan Jacoby, "Original Intent," *Mother Jones*, December 2005.

Adam Liptak, "The First Amendment," *New York Times Upfront*, October 9, 2006.

Colby M. May, "Religion's Legal Place in the Schoolhouse," *School Administrator*, October 2006.

Martha McCarthy, "Beyond the Wall of Separation: Church-State Concerns in Public Schools," *Phi Delta Kappan*, June 2009.

Martha M. McCarthy and Larry W. Barber, "Much Ado Over Graduation Prayer," *Phi Delta Kappan*, October 1993.

Barack Obama, "One Nation . . . Under God?" *Sojourners Magazine*, November 2006.

Jeff Passe and Lara Willox, "Teaching Religion in America's Public Schools: A Necessary Disruption," *Social Studies*, May–June 2009.

Sam Roberts, "1925: The 'Monkey Trial,'" *New York Times Upfront*, March 28, 2005.

David Van Biema, "The Case for Teaching the Bible," *Time*, April 2, 2007.

Charmaine Yoest, "The Four Rs: Readin', Writin', 'Rithmetic, and Religion?" *Weekly Standard*, October 24, 2005.

Index